LIBRARY OF RELIGIOU!

Edited by Mark A. Noll

The LIBRARY OF RELIGIOUS BIOGRAPHY is a series of original biographies on important religious figures throughout American and British history.

The authors are well-known historians, each a recognized authority in the period of religious history in which his or her subject lived and worked. Grounded in solid research of both published and archival sources, these volumes link the lives of their subjects — not always thought of as "religious" persons — to the broader cultural contexts and religious issues that surrounded them. Each volume includes a bibliographical essay and an index to serve the needs of students, teachers, and researchers.

Marked by careful scholarship yet free of footnotes and academic jargon, the books in this series are well-written narratives meant to be *read* and *enjoyed* as well as studied.

LIBRARY OF RELIGIOUS BIOGRAPHY

William Ewart Gladstone: Faith and Politics in Victorian Britain
David Bebbington

Aimee Semple McPherson: Everybody's Sister • *Edith L. Blumhofer*

Her Heart Can See: The Life and Hymns of Fanny J. Crosby
Edith L. Blumhofer

Abraham Kuyper: Modern Calvinist, Christian Democrat • *James D. Bratt*

Orestes A. Brownson: American Religious Weathervane
Patrick W. Carey

Thomas Merton and the Monastic Vision • *Lawrence S. Cunningham*

Billy Sunday and the Redemption of Urban America • *Lyle W. Dorsett*

The Kingdom Is Always but Coming: A Life of Walter Rauschenbusch
Christopher H. Evans

Liberty of Conscience: Roger Williams in America • *Edwin S. Gaustad*

Sworn on the Altar of God: A Religious Biography of Thomas Jefferson
Edwin S. Gaustad

Abraham Lincoln: Redeemer President • *Allen C. Guelzo*

Charles G. Finney and the Spirit of American Evangelicalism
Charles E. Hambrick-Stowe

Francis Schaeffer and the Shaping of Evangelical America
Barry Hankins

The First American Evangelical: A Short Life of Cotton Mather
Rick Kennedy

Harriet Beecher Stowe: A Spiritual Life • *Nancy Koester*

Emily Dickinson and the Art of Belief • *Roger Lundin*

A Short Life of Jonathan Edwards • *George M. Marsden*

The Puritan as Yankee: A Life of Horace Bushnell • *Robert Bruce Mullin*

Prophetess of Health: A Study of Ellen G. White • *Ronald L. Numbers*

Blaise Pascal: Reasons of the Heart • *Marvin R. O'Connell*

Occupy Until I Come: A. T. Pierson and the Evangelization of the World
Dana L. Robert

God's Strange Work: William Miller and the End of the World
David L. Rowe

The Divine Dramatist: George Whitefield and the
Rise of Modern Evangelicalism • *Harry S. Stout*

Assist Me to Proclaim: The Life and Hymns of Charles Wesley
John R. Tyson

The First American Evangelical

A Short Life of Cotton Mather

Rick Kennedy

WILLIAM B. EERDMANS PUBLISHING COMPANY
GRAND RAPIDS, MICHIGAN / CAMBRIDGE, U.K.

Wm. B. Eerdmans Publishing Co.
2140 Oak Industrial Drive N.E., Grand Rapids, Michigan 49505 /
P.O. Box 163, Cambridge CB3 9PU U.K.

Printed in the United States of America

21 20 19 18 17 16 15   7 6 5 4 3 2 1

Library of Congress Cataloging-in-Publication Data

Kennedy, Rick, 1958-
The first American evangelical: a short life of Cotton Mather / Rick Kennedy.
pages   cm.   — (Library of religious biography)
Includes bibliographical references.
ISBN 978-0-8028-7211-1 (pbk.: alk. paper)
1. Mather, Cotton, 1663-1728.
2. Puritans — Massachusetts — Biography.
3. Massachusetts — History — Colonial period, ca. 1600-1775.
4. Evangelicalism — United States — History.
I. Title.

F67.M43K46   2015
285.8092 — dc23
[B]

2015004724

www.eerdmans.com

To Mathew, Steven, Lebari, Elizabeth, and Bariza

Quench not the Spirit.
Despise not prophesyings.
Prove all things; hold fast to that which is good.

(1 THESS. 5:19-21, KJV)

Cottonus Matherus

S. Theologiæ Doctor Regiæ Societatis Londinensis Socius, et Ecclesiæ apud Bostonum Nov-Anglorum nuper Præpositus.

Ætatis Suæ LXV, MDCCXXVII.   P. Pelham ad vivum pinxit ab Origin Fecit et excud.

Cotton Mather in 1727 at age 65. Peter Pelham painted a portrait for the family, then created this mezzotint to sell to the public. Kenneth Silverman writes that "Mather seems to have been the first American whose portrait others wanted and bought for their homes." (Used by permission of the American Antiquarian Society)

Contents

Contents

Preface

Search the internet for "Cotton Mather" and you will get an amazing array of material — much of it about the Salem witch trials and most of that information rooted in one source, Robert Calef, a man who hated Mather so much, and portrayed him so wildly, that reputable historians discount most of what he reports. Calef created a Mather that people love to hate. Type in "Marvel Comics Database" and you will find a cartoon image of Cotton Mather as a threatening, be-muscled villain whose cape spreads wide behind him as he leaps toward you brandishing a glowing sword. The database offers the following biographical information: Alias: *Witchslayer;* Citizenship: *American;* Origin: *Human;* Alignment: *Bad.* A better source on Cotton Mather, Benjamin Franklin, warmly remembered Cotton Mather as a generous man eager to do good. Mather was, in truth, one of the most energetic do-gooders in colonial America. He was a family man much respected in his native Boston, a pastor who was considered a leader of the churches of New England, and a scholar with a transatlantic reputation. If it had been up to him, the Salem witchcraft problem would have been handled without hysteria. Before the trials began, he recommended that the girls who professed to be afflicted by witches and demons should be separated and distributed to good homes where their diet and sleep could be regulated. He also advised the judges that the testimony of the girls about what they saw was very weak evidence, and did not alone warrant the conviction of any of the accused witches. Aligning himself with most of the other ministers of colonial Boston, Cotton did not support the court's rush to execute witches.

Such matters will be more fully discussed later. Here I simply intro-

---

duce the theme by noting that calling Cotton Mather the first American evangelical Christian is a deliberate echo of an earlier book on Cotton Mather's father by Michael Hall titled *Increase Mather: The Last American Puritan*. Between the 1680s and 1720s New England was transitioning out of a narrow but deep Puritanism into the British Empire's broader and shallower Protestantism. Many scholars have written about how the loss of Massachusetts' distinctive Puritan charter, the fiasco of the Salem witch trials, the controversy surrounding the founding of the Brattle Street Church, and finally the struggle for the presidency of Harvard all drove New England through a cultural transition that integrated it better into the British Empire. Out of this transition was born the broadminded imperial Protestantism that supported the beginnings of a moderate intellectual enlightenment in America. Also born was something else, a Protestantism of a different sort, one that refused to be lukewarm, and one that is recognizable as a root to what would grow into the American evangelical tradition.

Increase Mather and his son Cotton were involved at every stage of this transition. Of the two, however, Cotton more eagerly embraced the new and expansive possibilities of a Boston more connected with global evangelism. Whereas Increase often preached harsh "Jeremiads" against the decline of Puritan society, Cotton was softer, more humanitarian. He preached more about Heaven's call than God's judgment. He regularly called his listeners to be daily filled with joy and embrace a moment-by-moment conversational relationship with God. "There is nothing," he preached, "that will bring you so near Heaven, or help you lead a Heavenly life, as to keep alive a comfortable persuasion of this, that God your savior has loved you."

During the years surrounding 1700 when leaders in New England were promoting what Cotton called the empire's "Protestant interest," Cotton wrote that people of "the evangelical interest" were looking to him alone as their leader. We do not want to read too much of modern evangelical perspective into Cotton's use of the term, but he increasingly distinguished Protestants of an "evangelical" lifestyle from those with merely a genteel faith. Cotton supported the generic imperial Protestantism growing in Boston for ecclesiastical and political purposes; however, he temperamentally could not preach so minimalist a faith. He was a maximalist to the point of exasperating even his friends. When Cotton talked of an "evangelical interest" looking to him as leader, he meant a faction within the Protestant interest that rallied to his exuberant call for a distinctively Bible-oriented, day-by-day relationship with a remarkably active and communicative God.

The evangelical interest was not opposed to the Protestant interest; rather, it enlivened it to higher purpose and higher values. The old City on a Hill was gone. Boston was now merely an increasingly important outpost of the British Empire. Cotton Mather saw his job as, in part, to motivate citizens to be better, while encouraging those of the evangelical interest to lead in public education, Indian outreach, prison ministry, widow and orphan support, African American uplift, care for transient sailors, and the love that held households together. Cotton Mather rightly believed that those of the evangelical interest looked to him as their leader, and he prompted action on all these issues. In this book, I will focus on Cotton and his self-conscious desire to tug against the slide of genteel Protestantism. Doug Sweeney has described the birth of the evangelical tradition in America as a "twist" within Protestantism after the fall of Puritan New England. In this book I will show how that cultural twist had a person, Cotton Mather, rallying those causing the contortion.

The American evangelical tradition is best understood as a populist movement that has been most evident to historians in self-perpetuating networks of people, books, churches, Sunday school curricula, worship songs, colleges, and religious organizations. As a tradition, it changes through time. In the Great Awakening of the middle of the eighteenth century the American version merged with other evangelical traditions in England and Europe. Today the tradition is being transformed as part of a global evangelical movement. This short book does not claim that Cotton Mather's life sets a template for the tradition; rather, it is merely an essay on the tradition's earliest American form in the decades just prior to the Great Awakening. As a tradition, we must also understand that it was not created by one man; rather, it coalesced around one man during an unstable transition in post-Puritan New England. Thousands of people and a large number of churches rallied to the way Cotton Mather articulated and modeled what he called an "all day long faith" and described as a way of walking "to the very top of Christianity." During the Great Awakening that soon developed after Cotton's death, those who had appreciated his work gathered themselves into a much wider movement: a movement identified mostly by appreciation for the exceptionally active and intimately personal God who was at work in inter-colonial revivals.

What Cotton lived and preached, and what people rallied to, was a religiously zealous lifestyle lived in the light of a radically communicative God. While others were increasingly living as if God was rather taciturn and humans were left to their own devices, Cotton lived and preached as if God enjoyed conversation with humans and was ready to intervene on their behalf, even in seemingly inconsequential matters. Cotton Mather's life was not dedicated to figuring out God; rather, he was dedicated to being attentive, to listening, because he was sure God is always communicating. Nowhere is the communication more constant, clear, and important than in the Bible. Around 1693 Cotton began to compile his most massive and wide-ranging work, the *Biblia Americana.* In it we find the foundation for a type of information-rich biblical enlightenment that was broader, deeper, and more collegial than the narrower, shallower, and more individualistic enlightenment of genteel British Protestantism. In the *Biblia,* along with many other works, Cotton taught that reasonableness, not rationalism, was the foundation of understanding. Reasonableness supported the belief that God communicated directly with humans in the Bible. Reiner Smolinski, general editor of the modern ten-volume edition of the *Biblia Americana,* has described how Mather sought "to synthesize, and — if possible — to reconcile . . . scholarship with his abiding faith in the authority of the Bible." Cotton believed it was reasonable to abandon himself to the Bible. Throughout his life Cotton was widely appreciated for exuberantly modeling a lively relationship with Christ that was grounded in the Bible, a life that resisted the genteel tendencies of the new imperial Protestantism and moderate enlightenment.

As for the scholarly shoulders that this book stands upon, I must first note Richard Lovelace's *The American Pietism of Cotton Mather: Origins of American Evangelicalism,* published in 1979. I believe it is still one of the best books on Cotton Mather. Of the many biographies of Cotton Mather, my favorite is one written from a pastor's perspective by the Rev. Abijah P. Marvin and published in 1892. More recently from the perspective of literature professors, the best are David Levin's 1978 intellectual biography of the younger Mather and Kenneth Silverman's 1984 psychologically-oriented biography that won the Pulitzer Prize. Now at the beginning of the twenty-first century, Reiner Smolinski is writing what will be the standard intellectual biography of Mather for Yale University Press (to be published in 2016). My biography here is meant to be something different than these. The virtue of my book is in its smallness and in its focus on the roots of the evangelical tradition.

My own relationship with Cotton Mather did not begin well. In the middle 1980s I wrote a Ph.D. dissertation about two of Cotton's schoolmates: Thomas and William Brattle. From boyhood on into their forties, something kept Cotton Mather and Thomas Brattle from seeing eye to eye. Maybe the sixteen-year-old Thomas was one of the bullies that made the eleven-year-old Cotton flee Harvard. Whatever the cause, the two most significant people in colonial American science, both of them religious leaders and humanitarians, lived at odds with each other. As we will see, the tension between these two men exemplifies the wider tension between a genteel Protestant interest and a zealous evangelical interest.

Back when I was writing my dissertation, I viewed everything from the perspective of the Brattle brothers and did not understand Cotton. My best opportunity back then to learn to appreciate Cotton Mather was in reading Robert Middlekauff's *The Mathers: Three Generations of Puritan Intellectuals,* a book that won the Bancroft Prize and helped 1960s-style academics to understand that Cotton was an intricate, insightful, and innovative thinker. When I was close to finishing my dissertation, I met Dr. Middlekauff at the Huntington Library in Pasadena, California. He was exceedingly gracious to me, and, by association, I belatedly gained a soft spot for the Mathers.

On another day at the Huntington Library, a couple of decades later, Reiner Smolinski lined out for me his plan for publishing Mather's *Biblia Americana* in ten volumes. This project has opened up a whole new international range of scholarly perspectives on Mather. At present there is a cadre of professors and graduate students uncovering new material about Cotton Mather at the Universities of Tubingen and Heidelberg, and across the United States under the inspiration of Professors Smolinski and Jan Steivermann. I am thankful to be part of that community of scholars, and much of what I have learned about Mather comes from dinner-table conversation with them.

Is it inappropriate here for me to tell you that I now like Cotton Mather? There are many excellent studies of Cotton that keep him at arm's length. Here I think it best to simply embrace him. His exuberance has offended many scholars over the last three hundred and fifty years and his lively accounts of angels, miracles, and even levitation have raised many eyebrows; however, those who knew him best appreciated his wisdom, and his accounts of surprising spiritual activity are mostly founded upon his willingness to trust the credible testimony of his congregation. Much like being a member of an evangelical church, to embrace Cotton Mather is to embed oneself in a social network of shared exuberance and knowledge.

A Note on Quotes

In the interest of readability, I have usually modernized and stabilized Cotton Mather's highly expressive use of capital letters, italics, and punctuation. I have also used snippets rather than long quotes. Mather is a roller coaster of fun to read, but it takes time and effort before a modern reader can enjoy the ride. My editors have also asked me to limit the number of quotes from scholarly articles and monographs. I have complied but the reader should know that no historian works alone. There is a very brief list of sources in the back of the book along with an overly short list of acknowledgments.

Walking Tour

A central idea in this book is that the American evangelical tradition can be traced back to a pastor and his congregation in the North End of Boston. There is a very popular tourist route in the North End of Boston called the Freedom Trail that teaches walkers about the beginnings of the American Revolution. Coincidentally, when tourists walking the Freedom Trail stop at Paul Revere's House they are also standing on Ground Zero of the American evangelical tradition. Revere's house stands on the site of the house in which Cotton Mather was raised. To the right of the house is the site of the church that Cotton Mather pastored. Given this coincidence, I add at the end of this book a guide to a Cotton Mather Trail.

CHAPTER ONE

The Last Decades of Puritan Boston

1663-1674

The Pastor's Study

Cotton Mather was a pastor and a scholar. In his *Diary* he thanked God for his "tender heart" and "active mind." Although his scholarship made him internationally famous, his deepest influence was as a local pastor. His whole career was rooted in a small district of Boston called the "North End." For decades, until the last five years of his life, he was what we would call an "associate" pastor of North Church. His father, the senior pastor, was a powerful minister not known for friendliness. Because of this, much of the neighborhood work of visiting among church families went to his gregarious and enthusiastic son. Cotton Mather's congregation, in general, loved him. When Cotton's exuberance took him into revolutionary politics, religious extravagance, and even the brink of financial ruin, his congregation encouraged him, defended him, and bailed him out.

Cotton took his role as shepherd of a flock very seriously. Aside from preaching, he organized and led many neighborhood groups that met on a regular schedule. These groups were often targeted: some to youth, some to black people, and some to specific collections of families. Cotton would also organize groups for a special purpose such as taking care of widows and, for at least a while, learning how to sing better. Cotton was also long a favorite guest preacher at other churches and public speaker on major civic occasions. As a pastor, Cotton regularly visited the town prison. Since the custom of the time was to allow a prisoner awaiting execution to pick the pastor who would preach at a special execution sermon, Cotton often was the prisoner's choice. At these

1

execution sermons, Cotton would preach an open-air, straight-gospel sermon, sometimes to four or five thousand listeners anxious to hear about "the wages of sin" and offer of salvation.

But as much as Cotton was out and about shepherding his sheep, the physical setting for much of his life as pastor and scholar was his study. In New England, pastors did not have offices at their church. The Puritan founders of New England had been insistent that a *church* was the fellowship of believers and that the building they met in was just a *meetinghouse*. So, because the role of a church building was consciously downplayed, the spiritual center of the daily life of a pastor and his congregation became the pastor's house, most particularly the pastor's study. This was where he kept a library, where he wrote sermons, and where he counseled members of his flock.

For most of his career, Cotton Mather's study was upstairs in his house on what is today called Hanover Street, around the corner from the meetinghouse on North Square. His first study was in his parents' house a block away across Prince Street. For the last decade of his career, the church rented an older house for him closer to the wharfs on Ship Street. There he had a public "study" on the bottom floor along with a more private "library" on the third floor.

Mather's *Diary* includes many references to these pastoral studies and his beloved collection of books. He regularly thanked God for his large and ever-expanding library. His *Diary* also includes many references to visitors who would come to talk, borrow a book, or gather for corporate prayer. His children and other young people were encouraged to visit him. Mather often tutored Harvard students in Hebrew and in the study they would read aloud to each other from the Hebrew Scriptures. When it became clear that his beloved oldest daughter Katy was not going to marry, he set her to studying the many medical books in his collection in the hope that she would become a doctor. Cotton's father would often come to borrow a book just as Cotton went to his father's. The two shared each other's large libraries. Pastors visiting Boston were always welcome to sit for conversation or silent reading.

The *Diary* gives us a lively picture of the pastor's study. Like many a pastor, Cotton had to shoo some parishioners out of his study. We are told he had a sign, "Be Short," over his door. But, for the most part, Cotton's study welcomed conversation. Benjamin Colman, who from boyhood through manhood often climbed the stairs to Cotton's study on Hanover Street and later to his library on Ship Street, wrote that while Cotton's fame came from his publications and his preaching, he excelled at simple conversation. His "wit and fancy, his invention, his quickness of thought," along with his heart and affections, "overflowed" when talking with his friends.

Benjamin Franklin remembered being in Cotton's study in the rented house on Ship Street. The seventeen-year-old Franklin, working for his brother, a printer, had come on an errand. Coming apparently into the larger downstairs study, Franklin saw Cotton's father, "very old and feeble," sitting in a corner chair. Cotton himself, who was at his desk, "was in the vigor of his preaching and usefulness." After young Benjamin had concluded his business, he was surprised that Cotton, as was his custom, engaged him in "some pleasant and instructive conversation." The two continued to chat as Cotton ushered him out down a cramped passage "which had a beam across it lower than my head." As Franklin told it, Cotton "continued talking which occasioned me to keep my face partly towards him as I retired, when he suddenly cried out, 'Stoop! Stoop!' Not immediately understanding what he meant, I hit my head hard against the beam." Cotton always liked wordplay when giving advice, and, as Franklin remembered it, Cotton, probably smiling, then said: "Let this be a caution to you not always to hold your head so high; Stoop, young man, stoop — as you go through the world — and you'll miss many hard thumps."

Franklin's story is a famous anecdote that reflects pleasantly on both men. Two other famous stories of Cotton's pastoral study are more ominous. When he was just beginning his career, he and his wife helped heal a demon-possessed girl by having her live in their house. While she was there, Cotton discovered that his library had a calming effect on her. She could sit and read for a good part of an afternoon as he sat across from her doing his own work. Satan discovered this too and demons would throw her into fits in order to bar her from entering the study. Cotton surmised that Satan hated the pastor's study on Hanover Street. Later in his career, during a smallpox epidemic, a bomb was lobbed up from the street into Cotton's first-floor study at the rented house. The fuse fell out and the bomb failed to explode. In the great spiritual war between the hosts of heaven and hell, it was obvious to Cotton that Satan thought of his study as enemy territory.

More than a spiritual battlefield, Cotton believed his study was a kind of holy ground. The Bible sitting on the desk, he believed, was a type of burning bush, a book from which God talked. Cotton viewed

3

his bookshelves as a heavenly choir supporting the primary revelation of the Bible on his desk. More than a room for reading, writing, and receiving visitors, Cotton treated his study as the place where he and God talked most freely. Of course Cotton believed in praying all day long wherever he was. He tells us that he would pray in his latrine. He prayed while brewing his tea. He prayed while walking down busy streets. He tells us that he had a previously prepared set of quick prayers for situations that would arise while walking in town. For example, every time he caught himself admiring a particularly beautiful woman, he trained himself to immediately pray: "Lord, beautify the soul of that person with thy comeliness." Cotton prayed everywhere. His study, however, was a special place for particularly intense prayer. He would go there when great matters were weighing on him — a dying child or a particular petition. He would often lie prostrate on the floor. His *Diary* tells us that he would put his mouth in the dust.

More than simply a place to lay his particular petitions before God, his study was a place where God's communication with him was most lively and direct. Angels came to him in his study with messages from God. The Holy Spirit would often overwhelm him with divine presence as he prayed midst his books. Sometimes he wrote his sermons while kneeling at his desk chair. Day in and day out, the Bible was God's best means of communication with him. Cotton would, at times, open the Bible randomly to let God give him a distinct message for a particular situation. Mostly he simply read the Bible every morning and evening to learn what God wanted him to know. Cotton believed that the Bible coordinated all the knowledge that filled his bookshelves. Daily, from 1693 to his death thirty-five years later, he worked on a massive *Biblia Americana* that would not only illuminate the Bible's teaching but also show how the Bible illuminated knowledge of ancient human and natural history. But just because God spoke through the Bible, that did not mean that the Bible was always understandable. Cotton heartily affirmed that the Bible was filled with "evangelical mystery." One expected mysteries when God communicated. In the *Biblia Americana* Cotton offered a witty little circularity: "the gospel is full of this mystery, and the Bible is not understood without it."

In order to understand Cotton Mather we have to understand the way he listened to the Bible, meditated on the Bible, relied on the Bible, and even wildly abandoned himself to the Bible. As he told young Ben Franklin to stoop, he himself stooped to the Bible. He went to the

Bible to trust and obey. We should start his biography with a picture in our mind: Saturday night during a cold March in 1685. The unmarried twenty-two-year-old Cotton was up in the small study that his parents had cleared out for him until he got married and had his own house. Cotton was not yet settled on a career as a pastor, but he was regularly preaching at North Church. Whatever he was going to do with his life, he knew he wanted to live for the Lord. The only way he knew how to live such a life was to radically embrace the Bible. In that makeshift study, most likely a cold room without a fireplace, he asked himself the crucial question: "Why do I believe the Scriptures to be the Word of God?" In his *Diary* he described what followed: "I took into my hands the Bible ... and presenting myself with it, on my knees before the Lord, I professed unto Him, that I did embrace the precious book, as His Word; resolving ever therefore to credit all the revelations of it: that I would love it, prize it, converse with it, as His: that I would be so awed by the promises, and threatenings and histories of it, as to study a conformity unto the precepts of it, while I have my being. So, I blessed Him, for His vouchsafing of this invaluable Word unto me."

There on his knees among the books of his start-up library he set the foundation for his life as a pastor and a scholar. In this he was not abnormal. Many a pastor-scholar had done this before him and would do this after him. What made him the first in a long tradition of evangelical scholar-pastors is the outward circumstances of this affirmation. Within a few years of this prayer the Puritan charter of Massachusetts would be revoked and the course set in New England toward a broader, more moderate, Protestantism. People of an "evangelical interest" wanting to find their way in this new situation needed leadership. Cotton took for himself the role of leader. He was not shy. At one point he noted in his *Diary:* "I am exceedingly sensible that the Grace of Meekness is very defective in me."

Home School and Catechism

Cotton Mather was born February 12, 1663, in the house of his maternal grandfather on a rise just beneath Beacon Hill. Boston was then a small but growing port town of about three thousand people. The house overlooked the First Church meetinghouse where his grandfather was minister. Standing on the porch of this house, this young family could look to the north, across a muddy gully spanned by two wooden bridges, and see the meetinghouse of North Church. The summer following Cotton's birth, Increase Mather, his father, began a long career as a minister of that church. Cotton would also become a pastor of that church. Visible behind the meetinghouse to the left was Copp's Hill where he and his mother and father would be buried.

The Mather family moved in 1670 to a church-owned house on what we call today "North Square." Today, as back then, the square is actually a small triangular open space. In colonial times, the high ground of the triangle was surmounted by a large boxy meetinghouse. When Cotton first moved there, North Square was the hub of fast-developing wealth and power. Several of the finest houses in Boston already graced the neighborhood. The Mather family, however, moved into a relatively modest house toward the low end of the triangle on the site of what is today the Paul Revere House. The Revere House is probably not much different than the house that Cotton lived in. The massive interior fireplace and chimney is probably a remnant from the Mather house, and the tight corner stairway next to it is probably similar to the one Cotton climbed as a child. A fire burned it down when he was thirteen. As a child Cotton would have often played down by the bustling wharfs just a block away. It was there that Cotton would have heard much talk of far-off ports and imperial politics.

Cotton was born in the Puritan Golden Age. Boston was the capital of a Puritan republic that had been largely left alone to organize itself as it pleased. When Cotton was growing up, there were three churches in Boston generically called First, North, and South. One of the distinctive aspects of Puritan Massachusetts was that they allowed only one type of Protestant church to be formed and called it "Congregational." The designation indicated that the congregations were independent of each other. It was important to them that their churches not be unified by a bureaucracy or hierarchy but only by a shared desire to be united in Christ. This kind of unorganized unity, they believed, was the way the earliest churches of Christianity worked with each other. In the Massachusetts Bay Colony those who wanted to organize as Presbyterians, Baptists, Anglicans, or Quakers could do so somewhere else. In order to promote the godliness of politics, the right to vote came with church membership and not merely land ownership. Ideally, in every town, the church was the gatekeeper to political power. For the most part, the system worked well in their isolated colony.

Cotton Mather was born in 1663 in the house of his grandfather, John Cotton, in the upper left of the map, just above where Tremont, Queen, and Sudbury Streets converge. Cotton lived in North Square as a boy, just left of the (B) marking the Mathers' North Church meetinghouse. From age 7 to 11, Cotton walked daily from North Square to Ezekiel Cheever's school (c) in the upper left of the map. Young Cotton attended there in the early 1670s before the Anglican church, "King's Chapel" (E), was built in 1688. Cotton's schoolmates Thomas and William Brattle lived on Brattle Street. Another schoolmate, John Leverett, grew up just left of First Church meetinghouse (A). After graduating from Harvard, Cotton moved into his parents' new house on North (Hanover) Street above the "th" in North. After marriage Cotton bought a nice house to the right of the (L). Beginning in 1714 Cotton rented a house on Ship Street near Fleet Street. The Mather family tomb is in the "burying place" on the right near the Snow Hill windmill. (Detail from William Burgis's map of Boston published in 1728, the year Cotton Mather died. Map reproduction courtesy of the Norman B. Leventhal Map Center at the Boston Public Library.)

Cotton was the oldest child of Increase Mather and Maria Cotton. Both of his grandfathers, Richard Mather and John Cotton, were revered founders of the colony, powerful ministers, and model Puritans. Along with his two grandfathers, Cotton's father and five of his uncles were prominent ministers. His mother was a daughter, wife, and mother to pastors. God, Cotton's father believed, often chose to shower saving grace on whole families through several generations. The Mathers and the Cottons believed as an extended family that much had been given them and that to whom much is given, much is expected. Throughout his life Cotton believed that God had a special plan for families as families, and he always tried to live up to the responsibility of being both a Cotton and a Mather. His father wrote that he had a "particular faith" about young Cotton. He felt assured that "God has blessed him, and he shall be blessed." Cotton believed this about himself.

Cotton Mather grew up in a loving family. In fact, the Cottons and the Mathers had a multi-generational reputation for being soft on children. Richard Mather, the first Mather in America, wrote on the importance of cherishing one's children, especially by talking and praying with each child individually. Cotton grew up in a home where both his parents went out of their way to talk to him and pray with him. David Levin's biography of Cotton Mather is especially good on this point. Levin emphasizes "the remarkable spirit" and mutual encouragement of the household in which Cotton learned to think. The love of his parents helped him love God. The model of Maria and Increase Mather encouraged Cotton to emphasize, throughout his life, God's love and mercy rather than God's wrath and judgment. Later in life Cotton Mather carried on family tradition by advising parents that "Our authority should be so tempered with kindness, and meekness, and loving tenderness, that our children may *fear* us with *delight,* and see that we love them with as much *delight.*" What Cotton experienced in his own home growing up he carried over into the pulpit as a minister. God was a good parent whose power was tempered with kindness, meekness, and tenderness. Delight should be the character of the bond between creator and creature.

The Mather house on North Square was a busy place. Aside from the pastor's study being there, it also housed a school. Puritans during the Golden Age in New England expected much from their individual households. "Look to your families," Increase preached. "Families are the nurseries for church and commonwealth." Massachusetts passed a law in 1642 requiring parents to make sure that their children knew how to read and write. Given the higher illiteracy of the wharf districts of Boston and the fact that men were often away at sea, Maria Mather's kitchen was the center of early childhood education in the North End.

The Puritan family was, in classical terms, supposed to be a household with arms open wide to all who came under its umbrella of responsibility. Maria, as pastor's wife in the neighborhood church, was a woman of great responsibility over many families in the North End. She would have taken in the children of illiterate mothers to study alongside her own children and servants. She probably took in many of the illiterate mothers themselves. We can imagine the kitchen of the Mather house bustling with women and children working, teaching, and studying throughout the day. Older children would be watching over younger children. Various people would be taking turns reading out loud. Children would be reciting their age-appropriate catechisms. Erasable slates would be being passed around for learning mathematics. Some of the servant children and illiterate mothers most likely were African, West Indian, or Native American. The North End was a diverse society. All in all, the Mather home school would have been a lively place. Young Cotton probably enjoyed the hustle and bustle of it. Later in life, Cotton's own household would always be lively with children, servant families, neighbors, college students, and visitors. Cotton had an amazing ability to concentrate midst hustle and bustle, and he probably gained this ability while growing up in his parents' house on North Square.

Cotton's mother, Maria, was most likely well educated. Maria was a pastor's daughter — her father was one of Puritanism's greatest pastor-scholars. Pastors' daughters were the most educated class of women in British society. Probably based on the model of his mother, Cotton had high expectations for women. He expected the women in his life to be educated, wise, and capable of participating in the family's cottage industry of ministry and scholarship. Cotton taught at least one, but probably all, of his daughters to read Latin, Greek, and Hebrew. He enjoyed having the girls with him in his study probably just as much as his mother enjoyed having him reading to her in the kitchen when he was young.

Beginning with reading and writing, Puritan education quickly turned to memorizing catechisms. Catechisms are a type of song, a memorized call and response between a teacher and student. They introduce children to precise information that society agrees upon. Similar to a catechism today is the reciting of the Pledge of Allegiance. A teacher says a set phrase such as "Place your hand over your heart. Ready. Begin." Then all children, using a united rhythm, recite a collection of statements. Catechisms are especially good for affirming traditions of knowledge. Two people at minimum, but the more the merrier, is the ideal of a catechism. One person calls the question, and others call back the answer. Nobody is learning to think individualistically or critically. Nobody is learning to think like a philosopher. Everybody is learning to think within a tradition of shared knowledge. Everybody is affirming out loud and in the same rhythm what everybody already knows.

Maria's father, John Cotton, published a widely used catechism called *Milk for Babes, Drawn Out of the Breasts of Both Testaments.* All of Maria's children would have learned it soon after they could speak:

Q. What hath God done for you?
A. God hath made me, He keepeth me, and He can save me.

Q. Who is God?
A. God is a Spirit of Himself and for Himself.

Q. How many gods be there?
A. There is but one God in three persons, the Father, the Son, and the Holy Ghost.

Q. How did God make you?
A. In my first parents holy and righteous.

Q. Are you then born holy and righteous?
A. No, my first father sinned, and I in him.

Q. Are you then born a sinner?
A. I was conceived in sin and born in iniquity.

Along with memorizing catechisms, children were also supposed to learn at home the skills of being "wise unto salvation." This began with training infants to be obedient, kind, and patient, to which were added skills of self-examination, spiritual observation, and prayer. As taught in John Cotton's *Milk for Babes,* children were supposed to learn that spiritual warfare wages within them and around them. Children needed to learn how to weigh both their holiness and their sinfulness. Infants were Puritans in training. Children should be encouraged to act "with all possible gravity" and be sensitive to the fact that their souls hung in a balance. God must choose them for salvation. In some children this could encourage despair, but it was supposed to encourage hope. God is good. "God hath made me, He keepeth me, and He can save me." Children were also taught that they were never alone. This would help them be good and also feel safe. "Dear children," Cotton's grandfather wrote, "Behave yourselves as having the angels of God looking upon you, the angels of God looking after you!" Prayer was taught from the first day of life. Young children were not only taught to pray but also to expect answers. God wanted a two-way relationship with each and every child.

At the Mather home school there would have been a time each day when young Cotton would have gone upstairs to the pastor's study to be interviewed by his father. Imagine Cotton as a six-year-old boy negotiating the tall steps of the tight corner staircase next to the fireplace. By this age Cotton had developed into a chronic stutterer. There have been some biographers, emphasizing a psychological interpretation of stuttering, that think that Cotton might have been afraid of going upstairs. His father was an austere and formidable man. Even if this is true, there was never a break between Cotton and his father. The two lived and worked side by side up until Increase died five years before Cotton died. If young Cotton was nervous going up the stairs it was because he wanted to please a father who had very high expectations.

As a six-year-old boy, Cotton was already showing great intellectual promise. Ancient languages came easy to him. Memorization was easy. He was fascinated by histories and stories of the Romans and Greeks. As the boy entered the pastor's study, Increase would have turned his chair to face his pupil who remained standing in front of him. Increase would then have begun asking him about any internal stirrings, any signs giving him a sense of his election to salvation. This would have gone slowly with Cotton stammering to finish sentences. Next he would ask him about his prayers. What was he praying about and were they being answered? At some point he would have had Cotton perform the Westminster Catechism with him.

The Westminster Catechism affirmed basic Puritan beliefs. It is easy to imagine father and son loosening up when they got to the catechism. Cotton knew it by heart and took it deep into his soul. He could sing the catechism without stuttering. Increase would have leaned back in his chair as he called out the questions. Cotton would have remained standing, happily responding in simple smooth sentences:

Q. What is the chief end of man?
A. Man's chief end is to glorify God, and to enjoy him forever.

Q. What rule hath God given to direct us how we may glorify and enjoy him?
A. The Word of God, which is contained in the Scriptures of the Old and New Testaments, is the only rule to direct us how we may glorify and enjoy him.

Q. What do the Scriptures principally teach?
A. The Scriptures principally teach, what man is to believe concerning God, and what duty God requires of man. . . .

At the end of the recitation, Increase would have been very pleased with his son.

Ezekiel Cheever and the Latin School

By law in Puritan Massachusetts, every town was supposed to provide a grammar school for boys aspiring to learned professions. The Greek and Latin roots of the terms "scholar" and "school" refer to the leisure time required to study, and future pastors in Massachusetts traveled this leisured path of scholarship. From age seven to fourteen or fifteen, college-bound boys mostly memorized the forms and declensions of nouns and verbs while working their way slowly through classical texts of literature and history. They would also be put on a regimen of religious and liberal arts–oriented textbooks that included a little mathematics and geometry. Multiple times a day each student would be called up to the teacher's desk to recite. The goal of grammar school was to prepare a student for the entrance examination to Harvard. That examination entailed standing in front of the president and showing that one could converse in Latin and was able to translate passages of Virgil and Cicero from Latin into English. The prospective student did not need to converse in Greek but needed to be able to work his way through passages drawn from the Bible and Xenophon. Most entering students were in their early teens, though some were only twelve. Cotton Mather passed the entrance exam into Harvard when he was still eleven.

Boston's Latin School was built in 1645 on School Street across from the south cemetery. From Increase Mather's house on North Square, it was a short walk through the center of town across the bridge, through Dock Square, up past Brattle Square, and along Tremont Street to School Street. The school was only one large room with tables and benches facing a fireplace. Next door to the school was the house the town furnished for the schoolmaster. Benjamin Thompson was the schoolmaster when Cotton first arrived, but he was quickly replaced by Ezekiel Cheever, who was fifty-six years old at the time. Cheever had graduated from Emmanuel College at Cambridge University before arriving in Massachusetts in 1637. Cotton Mather would make Cheever famous as a model teacher. Cotton's funeral sermon for Cheever in 1708 is one of Cotton's most influential writings on education.

It is hard to separate what Cotton actually learned from Cheever as a boy at school from what Cheever came to represent for him when a man. Laurence Cremin in his magisterial book on early American schools traces a distinctive evangelical thread of American educational tradition back through Jonathan Edwards to Cotton Mather. This evangelical thread insists that education should be concerned "not merely with understanding but also with the affections." Cremin titled it "Piety Rationalized." Citing Robert Middlekauff, Cremin sees the first flowering of American evangelical education in how Mather linked "the psychology of religious experience with the psychology of learning" and assumed that "the educative process is really an analogue of the conversion process."

Neither Ezekiel Cheever nor Cotton Mather invented a new form of Christian education. Both Cremin and Middlekauff can trace these ideas further back into ancient history. What Cotton Mather did for American evangelical education was to articulate powerfully his own experience in Cheever's classroom. It was there that Cotton found a teacher who taught his students "how to make prayers out of what they read." It was there that Cotton saw a schoolmaster who was not "so swallowed up with other learning, as to forget religion, and the knowledge of the Holy Scriptures." In grammar school Cotton experienced a teacher who wanted to bring children to Christ because through Christ all things become best known. "This," Mather preached, "was the study of our Cheever." Mather preached this in 1708 in a funeral sermon that was republished in England and several times later in American history. With the story of Ezekiel Cheever, Cotton created a compelling model that spread long into later history and deep into the evangelical tradition of Christian education.

At Boston Latin School, Cotton not only began a long teacher-student relationship with Ezekiel Cheever, he also began a long, tension-filled relationship with two schoolmates: Thomas Brattle, who was five years older, and John Leverett, who was Cotton's age. Thomas Brattle was the oldest son in one of the richest families in Boston. John Leverett was the grandson of a governor. Cotton was the oldest son of New England's most influential minister. Merchant, magistrate, and minister met at grammar school. Each of these three would have great influence on the future of New England.

We only have one story to work with from Cotton's time in grammar school, but it is a telling story. Later in life Cotton wrote that he "rebuked my play-mates for their wicked words and ways," and they "persecuted" me with scoffs and blows. Cotton took this early martyrdom to be a healthy beginning to a Christian life. Cotton also wrote later in life that his stuttering made him an angry person when he was young. From these two bits of information we can speculate that he was both self-righteous and insecure when he was in grammar school. He never quite rid himself of either of these two traits, and he was never quite able to be friends with Thomas Brattle and John Leverett.

CHAPTER 2

Cambridge: City of Books
in the Republic of Letters

1674-1681

Saving Harvard

Years before Cotton felt assured that God called him to be a pastor, he first knew that God had called him to be a scholar. His father and his grandfathers were widely considered the greatest scholars of their generations in America. Cotton described his grandfather, John Cotton, as "a universal scholar, a living system of the liberal arts, and a walking library." Young Cotton wanted also to be such a scholar. For the Mather family scholarship was not an end in itself. Books, in general, led to God. Throughout his life, Cotton lived by "the advice of the ancients: *If you wish to be always with God, always pray, always read.*"

Sometime in the late spring of 1674, Cotton, at age eleven, moved from Boston to Harvard. Father and son would have taken the ferry connecting the North End to Charlestown, rented a couple of horses, and rode for about an hour to get to Cambridge. While riding side-by-side, Increase probably explained to young Cotton that Harvard was an extremely fragile institution. The little college was technically illegal under imperial law and was financially near closing. Maybe on that long horseback ride to Cambridge Cotton's father told him that he was being enrolled mid-year, before the other students of his class and at a younger age than any other student, because Increase wanted to show his support for the beleaguered president. Cotton was being sent early to Harvard in order to help save it. Puritan fathers, in general, expected boys to become men very early in life, and Increase seemed to expect that his son become a man quicker than most. He could have easily let his son stay with his age group at Ezekiel

15

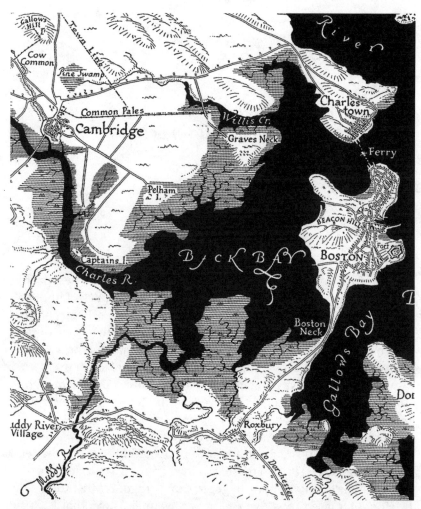

Throughout their lives, Increase and Cotton Mather often took the ferry from Boston's North End to Charlestown and then rode or walked to Harvard College in Cambridge. This route is the geographical backbone of Cotton's life. Cotton idealized Cambridge as an American version of ancient Alexandria, a "City of Books." Cotton found his first wife, Abigail, in Charlestown. Charles Morton, Cotton's most influential mentor, was the minister in Charlestown. Cotton served Harvard in many ways and in various capacities. Twice, when it appeared to many that Cotton was the obvious choice for the presidency, he was thwarted by colonial politics. (Detail from a map in Samuel Eliot Morison's *Harvard in the Seventeenth Century*. Used by permission from Harvard University Press.)

Cheever's excellent school. Instead, he pushed the stuttering boy into the uncertainties of Harvard.

When Cotton entered Harvard in 1674, the college's legal problems had not yet come to a head, but they were looming. Harvard had been chartered by the Massachusetts Bay Company in the way a modern missionary or oil company might create a temporary school in some outpost far from governmental supervision. Harvard did not have what we today call "accreditation." In the British Empire a degree-granting "university" was required to have a charter signed by the king and have overseers from the Church of England. An educational institution in America was supposed to be under the jurisdiction of the Bishop of London. Harvard had long been purposefully but unobtrusively trying to exist beyond the reach of the government and the government's church. Harvard awarded both bachelor's and master's degrees, but Harvard did not have the civil and ecclesiastical right to do so. New Englanders intentionally called it a "college" — indicating a housing arrangement — so as to avoid the legally dangerous term "university." A fragile word-game was being played in New England that could not last much longer. Increase Mather monitored it carefully. On the long horseback ride to Cambridge, Increase would have explained to Cotton that at that time, in the middle 1670s, the king, parliament, and church were increasingly interested in cracking down on wayward corporations such as the Massachusetts Bay Company and maverick educational institutions such as Harvard.

Aside from its legal insecurities, the college itself was in disarray. Increase wrote that Harvard was in "a low, sinking state." The college, he believed, was essential to the vitality of the Puritan City on a Hill. Troubles at the college indicated deeper troubles: "Ah, poor, New England! Thou art sick in the head and in the heart, and not like to live long!" Only twenty or so undergraduates and graduate students were enrolled that year, but most refused to pay tuition. There were no professors, only three young tutors. The president of the college, Dr. Hoar, was a good scholar but incompetent as an administrator. Students and their parents were calling for the president to be fired. Many disrespectful things were being said and done. Increase, we can be sure, told Cotton that he needed to be a model student, honor the president, and be ready to report back to him about unsavory matters. He would have also told young Cotton to obey and support the minister of the Cambridge church. But here too, Increase probably confided, was a problem. The pastor of the church and the president of the college did not like each other and were rivals. Cotton, listening to his father that afternoon, must have realized that he was being dropped off in the midst of an academic mess.

Within six months, as it turned out, the president was pressured to resign. Soon after, the college completely closed its doors for the spring and summer of 1675. During that summer New England became caught up in a devastating Indian war called King Philip's War. Harvard might never have been reopened if Increase Mather had not devoted much time and energy to saving the college. Cotton fully embraced his father's concern for Harvard and throughout his life was devoted to promoting its interests. Later, in the 1690s, when his father was trying to secure a "university" charter for Harvard from the king, Cotton published an exaggerated description of the dusty little college primarily intended for European audiences. "Behold," he wrote, "an American University, presenting herself, with her sons, before her European mothers for their blessing." Harvard, he declared, was a Protestant university, a "seminary of the knowledge of God, and a school for logical minds." The town of Cambridge was a *Kiriath Sepher* — a "City of Books" modeled on ancient Israel's academies in Syria. Cotton further compared the provincial college and its dusty town to Alexandria in Egypt, the intellectual capital of the ancient world. For the next five decades the Mathers, father and son, were Harvard's most active, ardent, and innovative supporters. Their investment in the college resulted in heartaches, but Harvard's survival remains the Mathers' greatest gift to American education.

As a boy, Cotton helped his father simply by submitting to being left standing on the decrepit steps of Old Harvard Hall. Standing next to Cotton would have been one of the three tutors who lived with the students and taught their classes. One of the tutors, twenty-two-year-old Samuel Sewall, would leave the college after the boy's first year, but Sewall would remain an elder friend and advisor for the rest of Cotton's life. Peter Thacher, also twenty-two years old, would also soon leave the college. The oldest of the tutors, and the one who was at the center of the college teaching staff throughout Cotton's years at Harvard, was twenty-four-year-old Daniel Gookin. He was the son of Major General Daniel Gookin, one of the Puritans most devoted to evangelism among the Indians, who that year had completed the manuscript of a handbook to New England's Indians called the *Historical Collections of the Indians.* The elder Gookin was a close associate of John Eliot, the Apostle to the Indians. His son, the Harvard tutor, inspired several of his students to learn the regional dialects of the Algonquin language in the hope of eventually promoting the work of Christ among the Indians. Cotton's father was never much interested in reaching out to Indians, but young Cotton, following the influence of tutor Gookin, never allowed himself to forget the Puritan ideal of sharing New England with the Indians.

By leaving young Cotton at Harvard, his father knew he was opening his oldest son up to many outside influences, but he was confident that tutors Sewall, Thacher, and Gookin would have a good influence. The college administration might be falling apart, the college president in despair, and the town pastor self-serving, but these three tutors were what Harvard was supposed to be about. Sewall became Chief Justice in Massachusetts, a major philanthropist among the Indians, and writer of one of America's earliest publications against slavery. Thacher and Gookin became ministers. All three were dedicated to Puritan ideals of scholarship, citizenship, churchmanship, and evangelism.

Young Cotton Mather clung to his tutors, but they could not protect him from the unruly teenage students who were trying to bring about the downfall of President Hoar. Two of the boys knew Cotton from their time at Boston Latin School: Thomas Scottow, fifteen, and Thomas Brattle, sixteen. Apparently they were quick to pick up where they left off with the young Mather who had a tendency to be holier-than-thou and had been charged by his father to uphold the authority of the president. The older boys apparently found it fun to rile the young boy into stuttering fits of anger. All we know of the situation is that Cotton wrote to his father in early July that he wanted to be brought home because some boys at the school threatened him. Increase complied. It is not clear whether Cotton went back at all that fall of 1674. What we do know is that Cotton's mother and father were very worried about his speech impediment and that the three gathered for prayer about it in the pastor's study in the North End house.

The Bible in Logick

In the spring of 1675 things looked as bleak as they ever would for Harvard. Students and their families were boycotting. The incompetent president resigned in March. In April the college closed its doors. Wanting to keep young Cotton studying, Increase, during the mornings

Harvard College as it was around the time when Cotton entered at age 11 in 1674. The main building was falling apart and would soon be torn down. Next to it, the Indian College was empty of students. Next to it was the president's house. The president was soon fired, and when Cotton arrived most of the students were boycotting. The college was technically illegal as an educational institution, and its degrees were not what we would call "accredited." Increase Mather, with Cotton's secretarial help, would take it upon himself to save the college and try to turn it into a legal university. Cotton Mather would become one of the college's most devoted alumni and wanted to become president and carry on his father's vision. (Harvard University Archives, HUV 2038)

of April 26 and 27, compiled a manuscript textbook titled *Catechismus Logicus* for his son to memorize. Here again, short catechisms such as this were more like call-and-response songs than full lessons. This was merely a little starter-logic for his son, but later it did find a place in the Harvard curriculum for the use of the youngest students. Cotton had a quick mind, and we can imagine again father and son in the upstairs study on Hanover Street. With Increase probably leaning back in his chair and calling out the questions in Latin, his twelve-year-old son sang answers back to him — without stuttering:

> Q. Inartificial argument is called what?
> R. Inartificial argument is called by the one name, testimony, and is either divine or human.

Q. What is divine testimony?
R. Divine testimony is that which is from God, and is the strongest
   form of argument, not having its quality in respect to testimony
   but the testifier who has the prudence, virtue, and benevolence
   of God on high.

Q. What are among the human testimonies?
R. Among the human testimonies are laws and famous maxims.

Q. What is reciprocation?
R. Reciprocation is when the thing argued artificially is applied to
   the testifier, and thereby argues for the veracity of the testimony.

As awkward as this reads, a foundation of social thinking was being established in Cotton Mather's mind that would always uplift the authority of the Bible, Christian tradition, neighborhood fellowship, and congregational life. "Inartificial argument" was an old Latin name for what we might describe as information known socially, the kind of information that a single person cannot think up by himself or herself but has to learn from other people in the form of books, maps, or conversation. In courtrooms, what the jury learns from witnesses is "inartificial." History and geography are the school subjects most obviously learned by inartificial means. In churches people learn from each other about God's recent activities by inartificial means. The events of Jesus' life, death, and resurrection are learned by inartificial means. Using what was called in Mather's textbook the "rule of reciprocation," the credibility of a witness's testimony depends more upon the trustworthiness of the person testifying than the seeming incredibility of the testimony. For example, if trustworthy neighbors tell Cotton — as they would later in his life — that they saw a girl levitate to the ceiling of her room, Cotton should not judge the credibility of the story based on whether levitation is impossible or not; rather, the credibility of the story is based on whether the eyewitnesses are conscientious men and women who can be trusted to tell the truth. Cotton knew of the levitation — the ascension — of Jesus in a similar way: by means of trustworthy eyewitness reports written in the Bible. By the reciprocation rule in logic, the appropriate first question should not be whether the event is impossible; rather, the listener should first question the trustworthiness of the source of the information. If the eyewitnesses are trustworthy, then the report should at least be entertained as probably true.

Increase Mather, while teaching these terms and definitions to his son that spring in the Hanover Street study, probably advised his son that there had long been philosophers who disparaged these rules of social thinking. He could give many examples to his son of theologians and scholars who insisted on thinking for themselves, by themselves. On the other hand, Aristotle, Cicero, Plutarch, and Quintilian had taught the necessity of learning the art of social thinking. They asserted that people think best in groups and within long traditions. First things first: an aspiring young scholar needs to learn the social arts of listening and appropriate trust.

When Cotton returned to Harvard the following fall, he continued to take classes in logic. Various types of logic were taught to students in a multi-year, multi-layered system of classes and textbooks. These logic textbooks were most often titled either *Logic* or *Dialectic,* or, sometimes, *The Art of Thinking.* The Harvard curriculum placed a high value on teaching "reasonableness." This felicitous term described something both bigger and softer than hard and narrow rationality. Cotton learned at Harvard that knowledge, like politics, was a fellowship.

Cotton learned in his logic classes that a lone and anti-social boy could be a great mathematician, a rational genius, and even a brilliant thinker, but no such boy could be the wise leader of a state or the pastor of a church. The most common analogy used for teaching reasonableness was courtroom jurisprudence: witnesses introduce external information into the court, prosecutors and defenders analyze the information, judges set rules of evidence and certainty, and a jury decides by consensus. Truth rises out of the interaction of many people. Jurisprudence — like the leading of a state, a church, or a family — was too important to leave up to a lone individual thinking rationally.

Another analogy for social reasonableness that Cotton learned at Harvard was the classical tradition of bee imagery. Working together, bees gather pollen (information) from widely diverse sources, organize the pollen in a honeycomb (a book or library), and, mysteriously, honey is produced. Books that gather together diverse information and libraries that gather together many books are "honey-producing": they are "inspired" in a mysterious way. Going to college was bee-like and honey-producing. Education in all the liberal arts, reading in the library, living with other students and the tutors was inspirational. Cotton wrote that he loved large encyclopedia-style books because each was like a "hive." Such books gathered together the thoughts of many authors from multiple books. The Bible was the greatest of all hives. The canon of books in the Bible was a honeycomb of entangled divine and human testimony that was uniquely inspired in such a way as to be "infallible." An individual using his intuition, mind, and senses could think with pure human reason and claim to be rational; however, reasonableness was social. At Harvard Cotton learned mathematics and philosophy and the high arts of individual rationality; however, he also learned that if he aspired to be a pastor or a civic leader, he needed to cultivate the social art of reasonableness.

Throughout Cotton's most important books he would always be careful to follow the rules of social logic. He became a great gatherer of trustworthy information and a consensus-builder of judgment. In the pulpit he upheld the Bible as divine testimony. In a book he titled *Reasonable Religion,* he declared that Christians are not reasonable "if we don't receive that book which we call the Bible, or, the Scripture, as a Divine Testimony." Note that Christians "receive" the book as a community rather than individually interpret, argue, or prove its truth. This relatively passive obligation was an important rule taught in the logic courses of classical liberal arts at Harvard. As we will see, it would be a crucial aspect of Cotton Mather's later leadership in crafting a "biblical enlightenment."

Stammerer in the Library

When Harvard reopened in June of 1675, Cotton returned along with five or six other students. Twelve-year-old Cotton again complained to his father that some of the boys were bullying him. Samuel Eliot Morison, author of the deeply learned two-volume *History of Harvard in the Seventeenth Century,* could never bring himself to appreciate either of the Mathers. He wrote of the year 1675 that "we may feel confident that normal college life was completely restored" at Harvard "if that insufferable young prig Cotton Mather was being kicked about, as he so richly deserved."

Whether the twelve-year-old deserved to be kicked around or not is questionable, but Cotton soon stopped complaining, and he settled in with the other students. Part of his settling in involved coming to terms with his chronic stuttering. He had to learn to live with the stutter before he could begin to rise above it. He struggled with Harvard's emphasis on oral examination. He could repress his stutter when he memorized oral presentations, but Harvard's curriculum expected students to be quick-tongued. Cotton had trouble in the debate-oriented classroom. He also could not keep up with the banter at the dinner table. Later in life Cotton confessed that his stutter was a "bitter cup."

Looking back on the lessons that stammering taught him in his youth, Cotton wrote movingly about having to learn to accept being humiliated. He was forced to be more passive than he might normally have been. Cotton wrote that as a stammerer he had to practice being patient, slow, and deliberate — qualities not in his temperament. He had to discipline himself to take the humble position of listener. As he learned these lessons he learned to fit in better among the bright, fast-talking students that surrounded him.

At Harvard, Cotton was happiest in the quiet life of the library. In one of his later books, he appreciatively retold a story about a European scholar who liked to lock himself alone in his university library. At Harvard it was hard to be alone in the library because the library in New Harvard Hall was the central room on the second floor of a busy building.

The construction of New Harvard Hall marked a new optimism about the future of the college, and the library at its center symbolized architecturally the renewed intellectual vitality of the faculty and students. Old Harvard Hall had been falling apart and construction materials for a new Harvard building had long been stacked behind the empty Indian college. Over the course of Cotton's first two years at Harvard, students excitedly watched the largest building in British and French America slowly being constructed, a building that would house the largest library in British and French America.

In the fall of 1676 students consecrated the new building by carrying the books from Old Harvard to New Harvard in procession. There were now twenty-two undergraduates at the college. Thomas Brattle had just graduated but probably stayed on at the college while working on his master's thesis. He loved the library and as a graduate student he would have much need of its books. Brattle also was deeply interested in architecture and construction, and we can assume he was one of the most attentive students to watch its construction. Thomas's younger brother William and their friend John Leverett were new freshman that fall and would have also helped carry the books from one building to the other.

It is pleasant to imagine the scene: Boys and girls from the community joining the students in a long double string, one string carrying books to the new hall, up the staircase, and into the second floor library, and the other string walking empty-handed back to the old hall where they would be given a new set of books to carry. In the old hall, taking books off the shelf, was probably Daniel Allin, a senior who would soon be appointed "Library Keeper." In the new hall was tutor Daniel Gookin, who was holding the title of "Library Keeper" at the time. It is safe to assume that Increase Mather was there too, standing next to Gookin, offering advice on the organization of the books.

Later that winter, when the snow was deep, we can imagine Cotton among the students gathering in the library after dinner. At the long library table working on a mechanical drawing is Thomas Brattle. Brattle would later correspond with the Royal Astronomer in Greenwich, and his meticulous mechanical drawings are today housed in the British Library. Thomas would long serve the college by teaching any and all who were interested in the higher reaches of mathematics and astronomy. Austere and scholarly, he became a lifelong bachelor. An oldest son, he was quick to point out errors and logical fallacies in the younger boys. His was the brightest and sharpest intellect of his generation. He was rich, well-read, and full of ideas.

At the other end of the library table, talking quietly together, open books in front of them, are the two new freshman from Boston, William Brattle and John Leverett. Sitting across from them is their new friend James Oliver from Cambridge. These three would be inseparable for the rest of their lives. All three settled down to live in the town of Cambridge. Oliver would become a doctor. The younger Brattle became the minister in Cambridge and was much loved by everyone for his humility and sweet spirit. Later in life Cotton would tell William: "You are a sacrificer." For Cotton, this was the highest praise he could give. John Leverett was the leader of the three. He had a cold temperament. People would remember him for his "authority." Cotton would later call him "that unhappy man." Leverett came from a political family and had his sights on law as a career. He ended up becoming president of Harvard, much to Cotton's chagrin.

Gathered in chairs close to the fireplace are tutor Daniel Gookin along with Grindall Rawson, James Alling, and Cotton. Each is trying to learn to read and speak Algonquin by reading aloud to each other from the Bible that had been translated into the dialect of the Indian "praying town" of Natick, eighteen miles southeast of Boston. There had been one Indian attending Harvard when Cotton arrived, but he seems to have never returned after the doors were closed in the summer of 1675. Tutor Gookin had been raised among Indians and would later become a minister in the town next to Natick, but he never became comfortable enough with Algonquin to preach without a translator. Rawson was the best linguist in the group and eventually became adept at speaking and writing in various Algonquin dialects. As a minister and missionary, Rawson would sometimes make a little extra money by translating English books into Algonquin dialects. Cotton was also a good linguist. He was eventually able to preach to and converse with some of the regional Indians; however, when it came to publishing, he relied on Rawson and others to translate his written sermons into Indian dialects. Each of these young men revered John Eliot, the aging "Apostle to the Indians," who had translated the Bible, preached and published Indian sermons, and even wrote a logic textbook for Indians. Huddled by the fire reading Eliot's Indian Bible to each other, Gookin, Rawson, Mather, and Alling aspired to be able to communicate fully with Indians. Most of the Indians they knew in and around New England could speak English better than they would ever speak Indian, but each believed it was important to learn their language.

All four would eventually become ministers and be lifelong friends. As for Alling, he was the youngest in the group and his father had recently died. Gookin, Rawson, and Cotton looked out for him. Alling received financial aid from the college, and was probably the student referred to by Cotton's son when he wrote that his father helped a fellow student pay his bills.

There were a few other students we can imagine in the library that night, but these mentioned here stand out in the history of New England and in the life of Cotton Mather. The boys in the library that night were, by and large, an impressive collection. Together they formed a scholarly community, a fellowship of books and ideas. Among them young Cotton found encouragement for his own scholarly ambitions.

Harvard also taught Cotton the quiet scribal appreciation of making notebooks and copying passages. Students were not given textbooks but instead were expected to make a personal copy of a textbook by copying one that was being passed around the class. Often tutors would create an "epitome" of a textbook, a sort-of synopsis like the *Catechismus Logicus* that Cotton's father had made for him. The tutor would pass this epitome to his students who would share it as they copied it into their notebooks. Students, fingernails dark with ink, not only spent many hours copying textbooks, they were also supposed to create their own set of "commonplace books." Such books were where students transcribed useful quotes from whatever book they happened to be reading. Ideally students were supposed to later transcribe these initial notes into much more organized commonplace books with indexes. The highest ideal of this classroom tedium was that, in the end, the student would have a collection of commonplace books that would be an encyclopedia-like personal information storage and retrieval system.

Cotton Mather loved all this scribbling and was a master at information storage and retrieval. He kept at it all his life. Cotton's largest and most complex books — his *Magnalia Christi Americana, Biblia Americana,* and even his more private *Diary* — are understood best as creatively expanded commonplace books. Cotton found it relaxing to fold, cut, and sew several large sheets of paper into a clean new notebook, then, in his precise and clear handwriting, spend an evening organizing and copying passages from published books.

The Eclectic American Scholar

On the walls of the library in New Harvard Hall were portraits of Bartholomäus Keckermann and William Ames. Both of these men had been educators in the Netherlands who wrote widely used textbooks and were great proponents of the Christian liberal arts. Scholarship in the Netherlands in the seventeenth century was at the center of what was called the Republic of Letters. Citizenship in this bookish republic required extensive reading, facility with classical Latin, and a high sense of scholarly fellowship and purpose. Keckermann and Ames were leading citizens of this republic. Their work as textbook writers was part of a Christian liberal arts movement generally described at the time as "humanist" and "eclectic." This educational movement had started deep in the early Middle Ages before the Reformation. It was called "humanist" because the movement recognized that God was ineffable, above human knowledge, human reason, and even human language. We humans on earth needed to be humble and accommodate ourselves to the fact that we see through a glass darkly. Classical literature was appreciated by humanists as a tradition of literature that shared in the weakness of our shared humanity. The liberal arts, in the light of this fellowship, were skills to help humans be the best that they could intellectually be.

Cotton Mather appreciated the term "humanist" but preferred the term "eclectic." In his history of Harvard, Cotton approvingly quoted a presidential address by his father when Increase Mather described Harvard's educational goal as "eclectic." Increase traced the term back to a sect founded by Potamon in ancient Greece "who, adhering to no former sect, chose out of them all what they liked best in any of them." Increase then declared that Harvard followed the tradition of the eclectics. Harvard students, he affirmed, adopted "a liberal mode of philosophizing," and he insisted that students were "pledged to the formulas of no master." He then recited the humanist motto of eclecticism: " 'Find a friend in Plato, a friend in Socrates' (and I say, find a friend in Aristotle) but be sure, above all, to find a friend in truth."

Commitment to humanistic and eclectic liberal arts was personified at Harvard by the portraits of Ames and Keckermann in the library. Cotton Mather drank deep from this distrust of following one system of thought. Cotton was not interested in being a "Calvinist." The Harvard curriculum did not teach "Calvinism." Cotton affirmed the Westminster Confession because it declared biblical truths. He did not affirm the theology of a recent systematic thinker named John Calvin. Cotton, when it came to describing his own Christian position, appreciated the label "eleutherian," meaning freedom lover. He did not promote himself as a "Calvinist" because that was too narrow and smacked of idolizing one human thinker.

Cotton never became a Great Thinker. He rarely aspired to be creative. In his heart of hearts he may have wanted to be a Great Thinker, but he learned as a student at Harvard to promote himself as a lesser thinker of the humanist and eclectic sort. He embraced the social methods of reasonableness more than the critical methods of rationalism. He affirmed the Bible's infallibility but not his human ability to always understand the Bible. He learned to pull back from, even distrust, systematic thinking. Cotton learned at Harvard to present himself as the humble scholar. Maybe the best example of Cotton's humility within the Republic of Letters is his novel use of the word "American." Cotton is the first person in American literature to think of himself as an "American" writer. He used the word in the title of his *Biblia Americana;* he called Harvard an American university; he rather freely presented himself as an American author. This might strike us today as pride, but "American," at that time in European minds, designated something provincial, something out on the frontier, something unrefined. Cotton Mather embraced the role of an "American" correspondent sending missives into the European Republic of Letters. He was a stuttering, humble, provincial scholar, anxious to share information from the frontier.

CHAPTER 3

Listening for a Call

1681-1688

Closure with the Lord Jesus Christ

A few months before graduating from Harvard with his master's degree, eighteen-year-old Cotton included in his *Diary* a remembrance of his "closure with the Lord Jesus Christ." The prayer probably harkens back to when he joined his family's North Church and offered public testimony of his faith. Cotton offered it to readers of his *Diary* as a "glorious transaction" in which he affirmed "a covenant of redemption" with God. After affirming his own belief, he stated that "never came a poor soul to the Lord Jesus Christ in vain, and I do believe that I myself should not find it in vain." As a result of this transaction he further affirmed that God would do great things for him: "Having been the author, he will be the finisher of my faith."

Unlike most of the prayers described or written in the *Diary,* this passage has a lawyerly feel as if two parties were sealing a deal. In Puritan New England it was appropriate and expected for people to be able to attest to praying one of these types of prayers. Paul in Romans 3–4 had used succinct legal terms and courtroom imagery to describe how God redeemed sinners. New England Puritans, following Paul's example, placed great emphasis on prospective church members being able to "testify," as in a judicial setting, to a "closure" that affirmed beyond reasonable doubt that they were one of the redeemed. Evangelical tradition would long promote the usefulness, for oneself and one's evangelism, of this kind of decisive prayer.

A Long Obedience in the Same Direction

The closure prayer is consistent with the tone of the *Diary* overall. What is called the *Diary* is Cotton's most intriguing and compelling publication; it houses descriptions of major events, his thoughts and beliefs, and his spiritual encounters. It should be considered a classic of evangelical spirituality. However, the *Diary* is a more complicated book than one would expect. He considered it a collection of remembrances and transcribed them on his birthdays into yearly bundles. Still, some remembrances do not even have a year clearly designated. Additionally, it was not strictly intended to be a private work. Cotton was planning on his children and even others reading it. In fact, it was never a completely private document even during his own lifetime. Ultimately, the *Diary* provides an expansive picture of Cotton's beliefs and experiences.

What we have of the *Diary* begins when he is seventeen years old, shortly before his closure prayer, and ends when he is sixty-two. Throughout this forty-five-year record there is a saint-like intensity in him that turns every day into a personal battle within God's cosmic war with the Devil. Those who have wanted to psychoanalyze Cotton have found the *Diary* to be a treasury of emotional instability. His self-righteousness sometimes oozes out when he yearns for humility. Cotton diagnosed himself as sometimes falling "under the power of melancholia." He regularly described himself in his study praying stretched prostrate on the floor. He often called his children and young people from his congregation into his study for spiritual uplift and was happy when such meetings ended with everybody crying. But the *Diary* is also filled with examples of consistent and exemplary Christian behavior. He recorded the death of two wives and many of his children in the *Diary*. Like King David, he prayed anxiously for each but accepted God's will when death came. Suffering is normal and expected in the *Diary,* but so too is joy. Year after year he regularly offered lists of thanksgivings, and the word "delight" appears often.

In *Cotton Mather and Benjamin Franklin: The Price of Representative Personality,* Mitchell Breitwieser notes the literary energy Mather and Franklin invested in presenting themselves as models to readers. Breitwieser describes the difference between the two: for Franklin, "the self is governor, the specimen of valid human nature"; for Mather, "the self is that which is to be governed," the specimen of a flawed human nature needing always to aspire to a higher, unattainable self. If the *Diary* is to be read well, it needs to be read as a tense, push-pull dialogue between Mather and himself. Cotton's internal dialog resembles that of St. Paul in Romans 7:14-25. There Paul presents himself as the sinful, wretched man that he is, aspiring while constantly failing, "a prisoner of the law of sin."

Philip Schaff, the great church historian, described regular Christian prayer as the "pulse and thermometer of spiritual life." Cotton's *Diary* demonstrates that his pulse was strong and his spiritual life hot. "My life is almost a continual conversation with heaven," Cotton wrote in 1713. The *Diary* models prayer as a way of living. Cotton's prayer life was marked by its core consistency, "a long obedience in the same direction." It is evident that from the time he was a young man, Cotton intended to present his life to the eventual readers of his *Diary* with warts-and-all honesty. Cotton wanted readers to know that he prayed himself through of all life's issues. As Paul called to the Corinthians, Cotton calls readers of the *Diary* to follow him as he follows Christ.

Angelic Encounters

Due to the nature of the *Diary,* it is not clear when or how many times Cotton encountered angels. His most vivid encounter with an angel is one such incident that does not have a clearly designated year.

Cotton used the term "angel" broadly for all kinds of non-human, communicating beings created by God. In the *Biblia Americana* he succinctly wrote that "we have reason" to believe in angels "because we have Scripture." Throughout the whole Bible there are "a prodigious number" of accounts of spiritual beings acting in league with God or with Satan. Cotton simply took it for granted that if one believed the Bible at all, one would believe in good and bad angels. Cotton also found people's experiences, including his own, as overwhelming evidence that angels were still active in the world. Cotton's father published an *Angelography* in which he, with the help of his son, not only gathered Christian accounts but also various non-Christian accounts of angels, including accounts by Muslims and North American Indians. Cotton took seriously the advice in Hebrews 13 that people should entertain strangers, "for by doing so some people have entertained angels without knowing it." He noted in the *Biblia Americana* that Homer also had written of gods disguised as pilgrims passing through towns and cities. As always, Cotton thought the ancient Greeks had a good understanding of the spiritual life of the cosmos; however, they needed the Bible to give them the full picture.

The Mathers, father and son, were dismissive of obstinate skeptics who refused to accept the varieties of reliable testimony about angels. Skepticism in general, they insisted, is understandable and even laudable; on the other hand, obstinacy makes skepticism unreasonable. Obstinate skeptics will never be convinced that angels exist, not because there is no proof, but rather because they are obstinate.

The Mathers were also disappointed with the increasing number of Protestants who chose to ignore or downplay accounts of angelic visitations. Protestantism has a reductionist tendency rooted in its antagonism toward what the Reformers considered the overblown spirituality of the Roman Catholic Church. During the seventeenth century Protestants often reacted against the myriad stories coming out of Catholic countries reporting apparitions of the Virgin Mary, levitations of various saints, and miracles of absurd proportions. Many Protestant theologians theorized that the age of miracles had ended long ago after the first few generations of the early church. God, they tended to think, worked in their day with more decency and good order.

Increase and Cotton Mather were never so reductionistic. The Bible indicated that God and creation were both lively and unpredictable. The book of Ecclesiastes asks, "Who can straighten what God has made crooked?" Increase noted in his *Angelography* that the Bible teaches the existence of angels. A simple emphasis on the Bible had to include recognition that creation was wilder than philosophers imagine. Father and son sent letters throughout New England asking for stories of "remarkable providences," and Cotton collected stories of answered prayers that reached Roman Catholic proportions of the miraculous. If the story came from credible and judicious eyewitnesses, Cotton was a ready believer. One of his wildest stories is an account in the *Magnalia Christi Americana* of an apparition in Connecticut of a distinctive ship floating in the air, sails full and gliding north, that was visible for half an hour. The apparition was seen by many and was the answer to the community's prayers requesting information from God concerning the ship's actual situation at sea. Cotton, following in the medieval Catholic tradition, was more worried about believing too little than believing too much. When confronted with a story like this, his first thought was not

"Why should I believe it?" Instead, his first thought was "Why should I not believe it?" Given that the story came from trustworthy sources, he was ready to believe.

As for angels, Cotton had an expansive view of their activity and role in earthly activities. Cotton believed very much in the Holy Spirit, but he tended to distinguish the more general activities of the Holy Spirit from the more particular activities of good and bad angels. Along with other people he trusted, Cotton experienced distinct encounters with spiritual beings both visible and invisible. Cotton wrote in various places, especially the *Biblia Americana,* that the main problem with such encounters is assessing whether the angel is good or bad, whether the angel is telling the truth or not, whether the angel is sent by God or by Satan. Many of humanity's woes are caused by misinterpreting or misidentifying angelic communications. Angelic messages alone, in whatever form, are not to be trusted solely because they come from an angel. There is never absolute certainty that one is not being deceived or that one is hearing the message correctly. Because of this possibility of deception and misunderstanding, Cotton believed that all angelic communications need to be vetted through biblical examples and teaching. The Bible as a whole is a stable authority, while angelic encounters alone are unreliable. Even Satan could quote the Bible to Jesus.

In nearly five hundred publications and many more sermons, Cotton never claimed any personal authority because of his encounters with angels. Nor did he ever claim a special relationship with God based on such encounters. We know only about one visible encounter with any definite information, and even then there is not much to tell. The meeting was a private blessing, and we know of it only by the undated transcription that he inserted into the *Diary* and later into the *Paterna* — his two most private books that were not published during his lifetime.

The note begins with an awkward heading: *Cum Relego, Scripsisse Pudet!* — "After re-reading, it is a shame to have written!" Below this heading is an unemotional, rather straightforward description of a youth to whom a winged angel appeared with a shining face wearing a white robe like those worn in the biblical paintings. The "youth" is twice referred to in the third person but is clearly revealed to be Cotton himself when the angel promises that he will write influential books that will be published "not only in America, but in Europe." The angel tells the youth that he will do "great works" for the church of Christ. The awkwardness of this third-person account is similar to the awkwardness in Paul's third-person account of his own epiphany in 2 Corinthians 12:1-6.

Given the double emphasis on his youth and the heading about an embarrassed re-reading, it seems reasonable to think that Cotton was transcribing a note written when he was around eleven or twelve. Back then he was not only beginning to have scholarly ambitions, he was also being bullied and was insecure about his stuttering and his future. The term "youth" in classical Latin is tricky because it does not have to refer to a child. Historians have read this note in various ways. However, it makes sense that Cotton, as an insecure boy, was blessed by God with an annunciation designed to give him confidence. Maybe he was in the library of the decrepit Old Harvard Hall looking at an illustrated volume of Old Testament commentary during those first months at college when he was friendless. Maybe he was there hiding from the older boys. Maybe it was there at the library table that an angel appeared in the shape of the image in the book and told him he would eventually write his own books of international influence and do great things for the Lord. After recording the event, Cotton folded it up and put it somewhere safe. Years later, he transcribed it at the beginning of a volume of his *Diary* — at a time when the predictions were starting to come true.

Accepting Vocations

After completing his undergraduate education in 1678 at age fifteen, Cotton spent the next eight years moving back and forth between Boston and Cambridge, compiling the work for his MA while also helping his father with his extensive correspondence, inter-church organizing, and book writing. His father was also actively involved with the running of Harvard and served, at times, as interim president during these years. Cotton helped his father as a secretarial assistant in all these activities while also beginning to preach on his own at various churches. When Cotton graduated in 1681 with an MA and no longer had rights to housing at Harvard, his father and mother gave him a room in their house on Hanover Street to make into his own study. There he could help with his father's paperwork, write sermons, and consider his vocational opportunities.

Pleasantly ensconced at his own desk in his own study at age eighteen, Cotton started compiling his own notes for his *Diary*. On one particularly happy evening he listed his thanksgivings. These included good health, comfort in his parents' home, a good salary as a long-term, visiting minister at his father's church, ongoing tutoring for students learning Hebrew, and his increasingly "well furnished" library. He was also thankful for what he considered a personal miracle: the ability to manage his stutter. He had received much help and advice over the years as he learned how to tame it. The best advice had come from Elijah Corlet, the schoolmaster in Cambridge, who had encouraged him to speak as if he was singing. The stutter never disappeared, and he would always have to speak deliberately, but he was confident that God had intervened to clear the way for him to take up the full-time vocation of pastor. But even with his stutter under control, he still bided his time before committing to ordination at a particular church. He wanted to be sure of his calling. In August of 1683, twenty years old, he studied the church records and counted thirty new members who had joined North Church during the last year when he was doing much of the preaching. He thought it "a probable computation" to expect many more that he would help bring to the Lord. Later that month he was on a pleasant evening walk, probably on Copp's Hill, the high ground where he would eventually be buried. He looked out over the North End and was filled with contentment that God had "cast my lot in a place exceedingly populous. I found my heart, after more than an ordinary manner, melted in desire after the conversion and salvation of souls in this place." It would take a couple more years before he allowed himself to be ordained; however, he was becoming confident of a particular calling for him at North Church.

During these years there were other callings too, other types of vocations for him to consider. Cotton was a smart and energetic graduate of the local academy, and he never easily settled into just one vocational track. Like his father he crafted his life to suit a mixture of vocations. He had long been interested in medicine. He was also interested in being a historian. These two could be easily merged into a career as a minister. He also yearned to be a famous scholar. He had no interest in "leading an obscure life."

Cotton also wanted a wife. He was anxious for one. He prayed to God "that I should have my bed blessed with such a consort given unto me as Isaac, the servant of the Lord was favored withal." For Puritans, living within a household as husband and wife, father and mother, master and mistress was also a vocation — a vocation ultimately more important than any other. In reaction to Catholicism and contrary to what appear to be clear statements in the New Testament, Puritanism deeply distrusted celibate spirituality and mobile ministries. Cotton Mather embraced Puritan belief that an adult individual's holiness is best expressed in a geographically and socially settled life of responsibilities that radiate out from the marriage bed to family, neighbors, church, and town. When ordained, ministers committed themselves to one neighborhood and one church for their whole career.

Finding a woman who would marry him was not a problem for Cotton. The problem was picking one. Graduates of Harvard were highly sought after by young women and especially the parents of young women. There was a tradition back in those days for fathers of high standing to bring their teenage daughters to Harvard commencements. The actual commencement ceremonies were interminably boring, but the speeches were only a small part of the picnic-like atmosphere of copious food and leisured conversation. Cambridge at commencement was overrun by the sons and daughters of ministers, magistrates, and the merchant elite. Everybody was encouraged to socialize. Marriageable girls — age fourteen and up — were encouraged to cast their lot for one of the graduating boys or young alumni. Introductions could be arranged, fathers could assess prospects, and agendas for future encounters could be negotiated. Marriage partners got to choose each other, but parents were seldom out of the picture.

Samuel Sewall, Cotton's former tutor and future close friend, was unknowingly picked for a husband by sixteen-year-old Hannah Hull when she watched him present his commencement address in Latin. Her father was not an alumnus, but he was rich — very rich. He brought his daughter to commencement in order to take stock of the prospects, and she set her sights on Sewall. Later she found a way to meet him, and only after they were married did Hannah explain to Samuel that she had picked him out rather than the other way around.

Abigail Phillips from nearby Charlestown would have also considered her prospects at Harvard commencements. She belonged to a prosperous family and could expect to marry well. She also had a sweet spirit that drew people to her. It is not clear who picked whom first, but Cotton was considered one of the most eligible of bachelors. Increase and Cotton, in their regular journeys back and forth from Boston to Cambridge, were often in and out of Charlestown. Abigail was sixteen and he twenty-four when they married in May of 1686. In the following years

Cotton proved to be a passionate man, and he loved Abigail deeply. The congregation of North Church also loved her. She embraced the vocation of pastor's wife, and the two became one of the great partnerships in New England history. In her funeral sermon, Cotton described her as "a lovely and worthy young gentlewoman, whom God made a comfort and blessing to me."

Healer of Whole Persons

When Cotton was young and his stuttering seemed uncontrollable, he began studying medicine as part of his fascination with science and as a hedge on being a doctor in case he could not function as a preacher. Both pastor and doctor were vocations dedicated to the healthiness of whole persons. The difference between the two boiled down to one being primarily a spoken ministry and the other a more tactile and chemical ministry. But the two vocations were entwined, and, as it would turn out, Cotton embraced both. As a pastor, his family visits, especially to poor families, would often entail examining sick members of households and prescribing medicines. He would often bring his medicine bag with him on pastoral visits. Throughout his career he compiled a large medical handbook that he later tried to publish as *The Angel of Bethesda: An Essay Upon the Common Maladies of Mankind.* Beginning with youthful experiences, such as witnessing the autopsy of his baby sister Katherine, through to the end of his life when he promoted inoculation for smallpox, he deserves the designation given him by two historians of science in the title of their book: *Cotton Mather: The First Significant Figure in American Medicine.*

Cotton, like most doctors, mixed scholarly and commonsense medicine in his book. He did not create remedies; rather, he copied possibilities from European medical manuals. For example, to a woman who had chronic bleeding Mather offered this choice:

*Two ounces of an infusion of *Hog's-dung* mixt with one spoonful of *Nettle-Juice,* and given Morning and Evening, is a famous remedy. Some add, wearing a shift, which has been wet with a strong decoction of *Hog's dung.*
*A yet pleasanter medicine rarely fails. A mixture of *Claret* wine and old conserve of *Roses,* and old marmalade of *Quinces.*

Often Cotton simply offered common sense. Children, he recommended, would be much healthier if parents monitored their diet and did not push too much "strong food" and "rank milk" down their throats. All people in general, he noted, would be healthier if they drank more cold water. Strong wine, he said, should be watered down, or one should at least not drink more than three glasses in a day. Cotton quoted Homer, writing that wine "dulls the noble mind." Daily exercise, he wrote, is essential. Walking is good, but horseback riding is better. Healthiness, he insisted, requires moderate diet, regular exercise, maintaining a calm spirit, and washing one's teeth once a day.

Cotton modeled himself after the ancient school of *Therapeutae,* or healers of whole persons. When diarrhea sent one to the outhouse for long periods of time, Cotton prescribed medicines while also recommending "self-abasement." One should use the opportunity to remind oneself that what is being ejected from the intestines "is not so much to be loathed as that which comes from the heart." When watching a baby languish in sickness, one should think, "Oh! The grievous effects of sin." The "transgression of Adam" passes into us all, even into a baby who never gets a chance to be fully engaged in this world. A woman in labor, Cotton noted, experiences directly the pain that God long before decreed for all women as a consequence of Eve's sin. Facing the possibility of death in childbirth, a woman in labor needed to reverse Eve's disobedience by saying, "Great God, I am thine and I am willing to be all that thou wilt have me to be!"

An important mentor entered Cotton's life when he was twenty-three: the Reverend Charles Morton. Morton was one of the most respected Puritan educators in England, a man recruited by Increase Mather to come to America in order to assume the presidency of Harvard. He brought with him a set of textbooks he had written and a wealth of scientific knowledge. Upon his arrival in America, however, everybody quickly realized that Morton was too famous to be president of Harvard. The bishop of London had recently shut down Morton's school in fashionable Newington Green. If he were installed at Harvard, then the bishop would almost assuredly become dangerously interested in the American college. Morton was therefore offered only the innocuous and unsalaried post of vice president at Harvard. Morton, a gracious man, accepted the offer and also became pastor of the Charlestown church, just a quick ferry ride across the river from the North End of Boston.

Young Cotton revered the aging Morton. So did William Brattle, who was named a tutor at Harvard that year. Both William and Cotton found in Morton a mentor of great wisdom, knowledge, and experience. Morton modeled intellect and piety mixed in equal measure. He was a pleasant man who attracted students and friends. He was like Ezekiel Cheever, except much more accomplished in the eyes of the world. Brattle installed Morton's textbooks on physics, logic, moral philosophy, and psychology in the Harvard curriculum. Cotton later incorporated Morton's ideas about physiology in his medical book. Relying heavily on statements by Paul in the New Testament, Morton believed that the human person is threefold: body, soul, and spirit. Morton and Mather agreed that a simple dualism of body and soul made neither observational sense nor biblical sense for understanding humans — or the larger world of created beings that included angels. To complicate things even more, they agreed that there were types of matter that were both physical and spiritual. This spiritual substance could be either visible or invisible.

Cotton, ever the lover of Hebrew, named the spirit in humans the *Nishmath-Chajim,* or "Breath of Life." This breath was a spiritual substance. He described it as "a middle nature between a rational soul and the corporeal mass." At the time, this was not a radical idea. It was biblical and practical. It helped explain people's experiences. People did not experience life in a way that distinguished between an embodied machine and a disembodied spirit. "There are indeed many things in the human body," Cotton wrote in his medical notes, "that cannot be solved by the rules of mechanism." For Morton and Mather there existed obviously one or more types of invisible substances in the cosmos. There must be types of "ethereal matter" or spiritual substance that explain magnetism, gravity, and many bodily functions. Mather did not claim to have discovered anything new; rather, he simply offered a name, *Nishmath-Chajim,* for a middle substance, one type of spiritual substance that helped bridge the gap between the purely spiritual and the purely material in human beings. He said he was willing "to yield" to a hypothesis that better answered the evidence. On the other hand, he was wary of those who simply insisted that this "ethereal matter" did not exist because they did not find it when they cut into a body.

The complexities Cotton saw in human physiology are best seen in his advice on epilepsy in *The Angel of Bethesda.* Epilepsy, he wrote, is indicated when the body is thrown to the ground in convulsions, "eyes distorted, the mouth perhaps foaming, the face with an aspect full of agony." Cotton noted that epileptic fits can sometimes be calmed by medicines, and he listed them in his book. Other epileptic seizures, however, are not so easily handled. Sometimes "rational spirits of the invisible world" can "strangely insinuate themselves into the malady." Good angels and bad angels find epileptics to be ready receivers of their communications. Those trying to heal epileptics should be wary of this! The epileptic should pray, "My God, save me from diabolical illusions. Let no devil now play and prey upon me!"

Cotton rarely approached anything with simple, boxy categories and definitions. Both he and Charles Morton were suspicious of natural philosophers who promoted simple dualisms such as mind/body, spirit/matter, and supernatural/natural. The only absolute dualism was creator/creation. Both Morton and Mather thought of themselves as observers of real human experiences that did not fit into rationally separate categories. The experiences of being a pastor or a medical doctor would not allow them to think narrowly. Cotton's own stutter had proven mysteriously to be neither completely physical nor completely spiritual. The Bible, their own experiences, and the experiences of those to whom they ministered opened their minds to wild possibilities in nature.

Historian of Demon Possession

In 1688 the Goodwin family was attacked by demons. This family of tradesman status was technically part of Charles Morton's church in Charlestown, but they were living in Boston and attending Boston's South Church. By normal protocol, Charles Morton was the lead pastor in this situation. Other senior pastors in Boston joined in support, especially the senior pastor of South Church, the venerable Samuel Willard. Initially Cotton Mather, the young associate pastor of North Church, had no direct role. The most prominent pastoral, medical, and legal authorities in Boston and Charlestown were the first responders. Cotton took up for himself the side role of the event's historian. Cotton, ever the diligent transcriber of eyewitness testimony of peculiar events, became an eyewitness himself. Eventually he became so involved that he had to write himself into his historical narrative.

John Goodwin and his wife were good people with six children. In midsummer the middle four children, the oldest of these being thirteen, all began to suffer extreme epilepsy-like fits. Their fits were of such violence that expert observers said it was impossible that the children were faking. It was the opinion of "worthy and prudent" Dr. Thomas Oakes that "nothing but a hellish witchcraft could be the origin of these maladies." Eventually there would be many eyewitnesses to the key events, serious men and women whose credibility and authority could not be denied. Cotton's short account of these events, *Memorable Providences, Relating to Witchcrafts and Possessions,* begins with a dedication that he would employ "an American pen" and not clutter the text with philosophical speculations. He would tell the facts simply in the manner of a historian.

After professional doctors had judged the children to be suffering from witchcraft, Cotton wrote, local magistrates then "prudently applied themselves with a just vigor to enquire into the story." It was soon discovered that an Irish Catholic washerwoman named Glover had the motive and the means for the witchcraft. She also refused to deny that she was a witch. Glover was a feisty woman who understood English but spoke mostly Gaelic. A search of her house revealed the kinds of handmade poppets used by witches of that era.

While magistrates handled the criminal investigation, a group of five respected ministers dedicated themselves to the work of healing the children who continued to be tormented. At one point, the ministers, under the leadership of Morton, gathered at the house for a day of fasting and prayer. The ministers prayed and fasted all day while the parents and others tried to help the children more directly. The day produced only partial success. The youngest of the afflicted children, a boy, was delivered, and he never experienced any more torments.

By this time Goody Glover had been arrested. Due process of law would be applied to her. Translators for her Gaelic were hired. Cotton noted that in court there was no proof presented against her that could convict her; however, she convicted herself by refusing to deny that she was a witch. Worse than this, she did not simply sit silent. She raged in the courtroom and engaged in all sorts of blasphemies. This rage was not damning in and of itself, but, added to the refusal to deny, it pointed toward her guilt. Pushed for more evidence, the court conducted an experiment: they asked her to recite the Lord's Prayer. There was a popular superstition that a witch would not be able to do this. Working in conjunction with the translator, Goody Glover could only partly say the prayer correctly. Also adding to the evidence was that the affected

Goodwin children collapsed into torture-like contortions when they were brought into the courtroom. With the evidence piling up against her, Goody Glover continued to refuse to deny that she was a witch. Eventually "five or six physicians" were called in to decide whether or not she was crazy. These experts decided that she was of sound mind. She was therefore convicted and sentenced to be hanged.

At this point, after the trial and before the hanging, Cotton brought himself into the fast-paced narrative of his history. He twice went to the jail to visit Glover. Visiting prisoners was part of his normal round of activities. As with any customary visit to a condemned prisoner, he tried to help her renounce Satan and give herself to Jesus. Cotton recounted that she insisted that she could not do it. She was bound to "her spirits," and they would not give her leave to convert or pray to God. She also told Cotton that the remaining three children experiencing the fits would not be set free by her death. There were others, she intimated, who "had a hand in it as well as she."

True to her statement, after her execution the fits continued among the remaining three children. Cotton records that in the house of a neighbor, Mr. Willis, one of the three children was reported to have flown the length of the room, "about 20 foot." Cotton noted that no eyewitness could actually confirm the flight, but none saw her feet touch the floor. Cotton himself was not an eyewitness to this levitation, but he believed Mr. Willis, who was "a kind neighbor and a gentleman." Later Cotton would report seeing flight-like movements of the oldest girl, Martha Goodwin. But he never found any good evidence that she was truly defying gravity.

Odd matters of possible levitation were not the focus of the event. What everybody saw was that the children continued to fall into torture-like contortions and twisted into impossible postures beyond any mere epilepsy. Woefully, their helpless parents tried to do the best that they could while watching the children's "heart breaking agonies." Two worthy ministers tried to help, but their prayers and Bible reading only threw the children into "wonderful miseries."

With the situation not improving by the middle of November, Cotton offered to take the oldest girl, Martha, into his house. The girl's parents were tired and exasperated and let her go. At that point Abigail Mather, eighteen years old, found herself the mother-mentor for a demon-possessed thirteen-year-old girl. Together Cotton and Abigail monitored and regulated Martha's diet, exercise, and sleeping patterns, while she and Abigail worked side-by-side performing the daily chores of a busy household. At first Martha joined in easily with the childless Mather family, but on November 20 she yelled, "They have found me out!" and she again fell into various extreme "frolicks." One week later, on November 27, the health of the children, including Martha, turned a corner toward healing after a prayer meeting at the Goodwin home. The meeting included Rev. Morton, Cotton and Abigail, several other pastors, concerned neighbors, and the whole Goodwin family.

Cotton could have ended his history at this point, but he instead decided to report more about Martha's experiences at his house while she was still demon-possessed. Healing her was certainly his and Abigail's highest goal, but he saw an opportunity to use her to learn more about the demons who possessed her. If, as all agreed, Martha was being manipulated by a demon, then Cotton should be able to study evil angels and their work through Martha's possession. Everything he learned would be anecdotal, but he would publish these anecdotes with his narrative, and they could help further people's knowledge of Satan's ways.

Cotton's first "experiment" was to test whether Martha could read the Bible while being possessed. The answer was no. "If she went to read the Bible her eyes would be strangely twisted and blinded." What if someone tried to read the Bible in the same room but out of her sight? No. She would "be cast into terrible agonies." For Cotton, this extreme antipathy to the Bible led to interesting possibilities. Cotton started bringing her various books to see which ones the demons would like and would not like. Could she read a book by a Quaker? Yes, easily. Could she read a joke book? Yes. Could she read a book that proved there were no such things as witches? Yes. Could she read his father's book that proved there were witches? No! That book cast the demon in her into agony.

Visitors would arrive, and Cotton could perform his "experiments" for them. Could she read his grandfather's *Milk for Babes* and the Westminster Catechism — two short books she had read as a child? No! Those two sent the demon in her into "hideous convulsions." Could she read a popish book? Yes! Once, probably when Samuel Willard, the pastor of South Church, came by to visit, Cotton offered the girl Willard's own book. Could she read it out loud? Willard probably breathed a sigh of relief when, no, her demons would not let her read it.

Cotton knew that his experiments were a bit twisted. He noted that his reading experiments were not really good tests for what devils actually could and could not read. It was a "fanciful business" that yielded only indicators and possibilities. Cotton recognized that Satan was a deceiver and might, in fact, be playing with Cotton's own brain. He wondered "what snares the devils might lay for us" in such experiments. However, after warning his readers, Cotton continued describing more of his experiments. Could the girl read the Church of England's *Book of Common Prayer*? Yes! She read it well and called it "her Bible." Her fits would cease when simply holding the prayer book. Mather noted that he and others were tempted to use the prayer book as a charm with which they could calm her demons at will. Tongue-in-cheek, Cotton told his readers that if any Anglicans wanted to be angry with him about this, it was not his fault. Such readers should get angry with the demons. He was simply reporting what happened.

Many of Cotton's readers would have cracked a smile at that last passage. Cotton Mather was seriously engaged with healing a girl and studying demons, but his seriousness was not without wit. Yes, a witch had been executed, the Goodwin family was in chaos, and in the Mather house a young girl was being used to experiment with Satan; however, for Cotton, absolute seriousness was never without a touch of humor.

Cotton's narrative has a happy ending. After the prayer meeting on November 27, "the power of the enemy was broken." The children turned a corner and their tortures began to subside. Martha continued to live with the Mathers until the following summer. She liked Abigail and Cotton, and she felt healthy and safe in their home.

Memorable Providences, Relating to Witchcrafts and Possessions was published in 1689, when Cotton was twenty-six years old. The short and fast-paced narrative, complete with the experiments, was widely read by influential people on both sides of the Atlantic. Cotton wrote it "as plainly as becomes a historian, as truly as becomes a Christian, though perhaps not so profitably as became a divine." Here he distinguished between his literary life as a historian and his life as a pastor. During his life, his most substantial publications were historical. As a historian, he was more journalist than theologian. He followed the classical tradition of speaking freely with his readers about his sources, especially the credibility of his sources. Herodotus, the "Father of History," and Eusebius, the church historian, had infused their books with pleasant triangular conversations of social investigation between author, audience, and sources. As a historian in the classical tradition, Cotton wrote with similar candor and sensitivity to weaknesses of evidence. He kept his eye on what reports deserved and did not deserve "benefit of the doubt." Cotton was affirmed as a historian by *Memorable Providences.* It was his first internationally influential publication.

Some who read Cotton's book refused to believe that Satan was attacking the Goodwin family. Cotton called the refusal to believe the courts, experts, and credible eyewitnesses "the Sadducism of this debauched age." Sadducees in the New Testament refused to believe accounts of angels and spirits, and the contemporaries Cotton described as Sadducees were the increasing number of thinkers who were more worried about believing too much than believing too little. They found comfort in a simpler, narrower, and more logical cosmos than the one that their neighbors experienced.

A decade later a merchant named Robert Calef took aim at what he perceived to be Cotton's gullibility and made fun of passages in *Memorable Providences.* One in particular was a scene in which Cotton described how Martha would cry out in pain when an invisible chain was wrapped tightly around her by demons. Cotton had written that "once I did with my own hand knock it off." Calef laughed at the idea of an invisible chain and the notion that Cotton could actually believe he had somehow cut it off the girl. Calef was a Sadducee. He had a narrow view of reality and pitted his own intellectual categories against the experiences of a young girl and the community of eyewitnesses who participated in healing the Goodwin children.

During the decade following the Goodwin children's possession, Puritanism was losing its dominance and New England changed radically as it went through political revolution and the debilitating Salem witch trials. Through it all, Cotton became increasingly influential as people rallied to the consistency of his biblical focus.

CHAPTER 4

Entanglements of Church and State

1688-1698

Friendships, Fellowship, and Neighbors

Abigail Mather's family was of the richer sort, and Cotton was not uncomfortable among the wealthier and more powerful citizens of Boston. With her family's help, in 1688 Cotton and Abigail were able to buy a house in Boston's North End that was much larger and nicer than Cotton's parents' house. If we accept the drawing of the house and the research in *Stark's Antique Views of ye Towne of Boston*, we can assume that the young couple remodeled it in the modern style of the upscale Foster-Hutchinson house that was built around the corner on Garden Court by one of North Church's stalwart parishioners. Cotton's was an impressive house. He bought the house from, and later sold the house to, ship captains of wealth and prestige, and with it he and Abigail expressed the economic, political, and religious aspirations of their neighborhood.

The 1680s was a turning point in the architecture and mentality of British America. The clustered chimneys, random windows, and second-floor overhangs of Tudor architecture were giving way to the calm symmetry of what would later be called Georgian architecture. The street Cotton and Abigail lived on would be renamed "Hanover," the family name of Cotton's beloved King George I. Cotton Mather would eventually start wearing a wig as the older preference for long flowing hair on men gave way to the more hygienic coiffure of what would eventually be called "The Enlightenment." Samuel Sewall, Cotton's college tutor and long-time friend, was much put out by the vanity of young Mather donning a wig. He and Increase Mather would proudly wear their hair

The Foster-Hutchinson house (above) and the Cotton Mather house (below). The Foster-Hutchinson house was built between1689 and 1692 on Garden Court behind the North Church meetinghouse. At the time it represented the domestic architecture of the better sort in London. The tall pilasters were ordered from England along with much of the other finery. Abbot Lowell Cummings's article on the Foster-Hutchinson house is an excellent introduction to Cotton Mather's neighborhood and wealthy parishioners. Documentation for the house Cotton Mather lived in on Hanover Street is weak, but this drawing is well attested in *Stark's Antique Views of ye Towne of Boston*. The unsymmetrical placement of the chimneys indicates the exterior of the house was heavily remodeled to imitate the Foster-Hutchinson house. The pilasters, balustrade, and symmetrical window fenestration indicate London-style aspirations similar to the Foster-Hutchinson house. The elaborate door-surround was mostly likely added later after Cotton moved out in 1714.

long and oily for the rest of their lives. Cotton was in transition; Boston was in transition. The new North Square meetinghouse, rebuilt after the fire of 1676, was still staunchly Puritan in its boxy antagonism to outward show; however, all around it the North Square's architecture was beginning to take on the well-proportioned dignity modeled in London's more fashionable neighborhoods.

In the 1680s and 90s, Boston's North Square was the most concentrated center of wealth and fashion in British America. The growth of the empire after 1660 had served to make many an American ship owner and ship captain rich. Shipping money went into land speculation in the city and out onto the frontier. North Square became the most important colonial nexus for far-flung, transatlantic and inland, investments. Families living in North Square were often closely linked through systems of loans and debts with similar upscale families in Britain. The congregation that employed the Mathers was probably the largest and richest Protestant congregation in America. They not only took great pride in being up-to-date with British fashion and intellect, they also deeply believed that God was doing great things among them.

The North End congregation prospered spiritually under the leadership of Increase and Cotton. In the second half of the 1680s Increase Mather had become one of the leading figures of New England. After 1686 Increase served both as the President of Harvard College and as the senior pastor of North Church. From 1688 to 1692 Increase was the colony's political representative in London. With his father having broad duties and reasons to be absent, young Cotton focused his attention on the congregation, who, truth be told, liked him better than his father.

The North End neighborhood appreciated how Cotton preached practical sermons that inspired them to try to be better Christians. Given his congregation's maritime experiences, Cotton often preached with an eye on sailors and captains. Although he never sailed much himself, he published books designed to be read aloud at sea. In *The Sailor's Companion and Counselor* Cotton reminded captains that they were charged with promoting the faith on board their ships. A crew should be like a family and a captain like a father. For the less religiously articulate of the captains, Cotton wrote an expanded, sailor-oriented version of The Lord's Prayer for them to recite with their crew. In *The Religious Mariner* he noted that Jesus chose a company of sailors to be his disciples. Cotton proceeded to wax eloquent that seafaring people should be

Increase Mather, the formidable father of Cotton Mather who was called by some "the Mohammad of Massachusetts" because of his great influence over both the ecclesiastical and the political affairs of the colony. Michael G. Hall titled his biography of him: *The Last American Puritan.* Cotton revered his father and was his secretary and associate pastor for most of his career. Both Increase and Cotton were energetic scholars who wrote copiously on matters of science, religion, and history. Cotton was a good partner to his austere father in the ministry of North Church. Cotton was more friendly, gregarious, and sympathetic. While Increase late in life tended to preach prophetically against the decline of Puritan values,

Cotton was more encouraging, always directing listeners up to their Christian calling. This oil portrait was painted by Jan van der Spriett in 1688 when Mather was President of Harvard College and on a diplomatic mission to England. (Used by permission of the Massachusetts Historical Society.)

God-fearing people, that they should steer clear of the rocks and shoals of sin, they should repent and pump sin out of their bilges, they should bear away from lewdness, they should allow no false reckoning while navigating toward eternity, they should put ashore on the mercy of God, all this so that their souls might eventually be well anchored.

Cotton was also personable and sympathetic. People appreciated how in his sermons he reached deeply into his own experiences to draw lessons for the congregation. Soon after the death of his first baby, Cotton preached on the death of infants. The sermon was published in London in 1689 as *Right Thoughts in Sad Hours.* In this deeply empathetic sermon Cotton had little concern for rigorous Calvinism. The sermon was designed to comfort those who, like his wife sitting in the audience, had recently watched a baby die. "We shall see the dear lambs again," Mather affirmed. "Those dear children are gone from your kind arms unto the sweet bosom of Jesus. And this is by far the best of all, to have children, this day in heaven."

Increase was an austere man, but he and Cotton worked well together. They complemented each other, and their church appreciated them both. At one point in 1686-1687 when it appeared that the town,

church, and college of Cambridge were wooing both Mathers to leave
North Church and work instead in Cambridge, the congregation of
North Church responded by sending a curt letter to Cambridge declaring that they had prior claim to both ministers. North Church, using the
feminine imagery of New Testament churches, declared that they would
"be glad to help a sister that has no breasts, yet we see not what rule of
charity or reason, requires us to cut off our own breasts, that our sister
may be supplied." This feminine image of the nurturing Mathers, both
of them much protected and cherished by their congregation, remains
fundamentally applicable throughout their long careers as pastors to
the North End.

When Increase Mather began his four-year diplomatic mission to
England in 1688, his absence allowed Cotton to fully develop as a pastor.
He loved writing sermons and could have happily stayed holed-up in his
study; however, he also loved people and wanted to be out and about
encouraging them during the week. Visiting families was, of course, his
normal duty, but he went further. On his walks he would see groups of
people working side-by-side — women doing laundry or baking, sailors mending nets or rigging, rope-makers and boat-builders — and he
encouraged them to turn their shared labor into Christian fellowship,
singing psalms together, praying for one another, socially delighting in
one another in the Lord.

Soon after his father left, Cotton began organizing small groups
for the purpose of mid-week prayer and Scripture reading. Cotton had
a genius for empowering grassroots prayer groups based on intimate
fellowship and mutual accountability. As pastor, Cotton would attend
when he could, but the vitality of the meetings depended upon lay leadership. Maybe it was because he was only an associate pastor under
the authority of his father, but for whatever reason, Cotton was not
an authoritarian and was in fact very democratic and egalitarian. He
embraced the most fundamental notion of the Congregationalist system of churches — Jesus' promise in Matthew 18: "For wherever two or
three are gathered together in my name, I am there in their midst." The
Puritans had long encouraged regular meetings among pastors, and
they highly valued conversation as a means of attaining mutual unity
and spiritual betterment. Pastors told each other that they should not
be loners and that their fellowship represented the fellowship of their
churches. But Cotton pushed these ideas fully into the life of his people. He insisted that congregational families should gather in mutual

support and it did not matter if the pastor was there or not. As much as he revered the pulpit and was proud of preaching to fifteen hundred people every Sunday, Cotton Mather was a populist-style pastor who believed it to be his job to encourage his congregation to practice their faith all week long in the intimacy of their homes and neighborhoods.

April 18, 1689: Eleutherians in Revolt

Small groups of families and friends never confine themselves to just prayer and Bible study. There are matters of life and politics to be discussed, and Cotton's grassroots prayer groups were also grassroots political action networks. In the winter and spring of 1688-1689, there was much politics to discuss. Back in the middle 1680s New England had experienced what Cotton called the "shipwreck of charters." In 1686 Boston had received official notification that the Massachusetts charter had been revoked along with other colonial charters in New England. These "charters" were like corporate licenses and gave the Puritans freedom to develop their own republican systems of government. For fifty years the citizens of Massachusetts had shared a high sense of freedom and independence that included the right to elect their own representatives who, in turn, elected their governors. Under these charters private property was distributed, sold, registered, and protected. Congregationalist churches were also integrated into the republican systems, and citizens were encouraged to believe that they were building a model Christian society. When the charters were revoked, their ships of state crashed into the rocks. Everybody began asking whether families would lose their property, whether voting rights would be protected, whether representative government would continue, and whether a bishop would be sent by the king to rule over the churches and college, and no one knew the answers.

Fears about what might happen, and anger about what had happened, were focused on the new royal governor, Edmund Andros, and the people who had accompanied him from England. Cotton later described these men as "rapacious animals" and wrote that it was their fault that the colony turned against their rule. On April 18, 1689, the citizens of Boston revolted, not as a violent mob but as participants in a well-orchestrated coup d'état. The royal governor was arrested and immediately a previous governor was set up in his place surrounded by the leading ministers, magistrates, and merchants of the colony. Cotton Mather was at the center of the insurgency, and scholars have long noted that his writings during and after are the first clear statements by an American of what later would be principles of the American Revolution.

Cotton Mather first became an insurgent against the government when he helped to smuggle his father out of New England. Increase Mather had been commissioned somewhat illegally to represent the colony's grievances to the king. The royal governor was adamantly opposed and ordered his arrest. In order to sneak out of Boston, late in the evening of March 30, 1688, Increase, disguised in a wig, left his house, walked down Prince Street, and crossed over to Charlestown on the ferry. There he hid in Cotton's father-in-law's house until fleeing a little further to the north shore of the Mystic River. On April 3, Cotton and a group of helpers that included ministers and laymen slipped out of Boston undetected to meet with Increase. Cotton brought with him his younger brother Samuel, who would be his father's assistant in England. Together they helped Increase and Samuel board a small ketch that would take them to rendezvous with a ship leaving soon for England.

The operation succeeded in evading the governor's royal guard and no guns were fired. We can be confident that neither the Mathers nor the other ministers involved carried guns because that was not their way of leadership. They were ready to fight and die for a cause, but not kill for one. Back in the summer of 1685 Increase had preached, and Cotton had underlined in his sermon notes, "The ministers of God must then stand in the forefront of battle, and be the first that shall be shot down." In the winter and spring of 1689 Cotton was fully engaged in battle, not with a gun but with a pen. Somehow, assuredly by illegal means, Cotton got hold of private letters between associates of the governor. Cotton copied and published scathing passages such as one that described New Englanders as a "perverse people" amenable only to force. A warrant for Cotton's arrest was issued, but friends on the governor's council were able to obstruct the arrest.

Finally, on April 18, 1689, Bostonians took captive the governor, some of his associates, and the captain of a warship in the harbor. The leaders of the coup then announced themselves as a provisional government under the leadership of the much respected former Puritan governor, Simon Bradstreet. As crowds began to gather around the Boston

Town Hall and the possibility of a mob presented itself at the same site that would later be bloodied by the Boston Massacre, the provisional government issued a *Declaration of the Gentlemen, Merchants, and Inhabitants of Boston and the County Adjacent* that was read to a crowd and passed around the city and region as a broadside. The *Declaration* insisted that Bostonians were loyal servants of the king who were, in taking the governor prisoner, merely maintaining their normal rights as Englishmen. Although large numbers of armed men roamed threateningly throughout Boston that day, the revolution was bloodless. As it turned out, King James II in England had been similarly rousted out of England that April in what is called the Glorious Revolution. Boston's local revolution paled in importance and seemed irrelevant in comparison. In the end, all worked out well for everybody except James II and the House of Stuart.

Even though all turned out well in Boston and no one suffered retribution for overthrowing the king's representative, things could have gone the other way. Cotton Mather risked his freedom, maybe even his life, in what could have been prosecuted as an act of treason. There is ample evidence that he was the primary author of the *Declaration of the Gentlemen.* Certainly he was active with his pen at the most critical time and place. Edward Randolph, one of those arrested with the governor, reported that he saw Cotton Mather writing at a desk in the background when he was forced to stand before his captors. Randolph named the twenty-six-year-old Mather, along with six other Boston clergy, as serving among the "chief designers" of the revolution. Cotton offered support for the assertion that he was one of the thinkers behind the revolution by publishing his political views in biographical sketches of two governors: Simon Bradstreet and William Phips. These essays were widely read in Britain and America over the next century and promoted what would be the essential values of the American Revolution. In them he bemoaned the unchecked power of the royal governor and his tyrannical measures: his dissolution of a representative legislature, taxation without representation, undermining of property rights, and various impositions showing disdain for the rights and freedoms of American churches, towns, and individuals. Cotton Mather was willing to risk his life and liberty to defend the rights of English citizens not just because he was British, but also because he believed that the republican values of the British Constitution were biblical.

One of the lesser-told stories of the Bible is the account of Joseph conniving in the service of Pharaoh to undermine the freedom of the people of Egypt by creating a situation that forced the people to sell themselves and their families into slavery. Joseph, smart and tricky servant of the king that he was, accomplished this in such a way that the people of Egypt not only did not revolt, but thankfully embraced their bondage to Pharaoh. Here and in the story of the people of Israel calling on Samuel to ask God for a king, Cotton Mather joined with many political thinkers of his era in seeing resonance in the stories about the fickleness of the people allowing themselves to fall into slavery, the dangers of concentrating power into an arbitrary monarchy, and the wisdom of dispersing power out to a senate. Assemblies of the people were important for good government, but the fickleness of democracy needed to be held in check by an oligarchical branch of government. Overarching all are the godly pursuit of earthly happiness and the divine assistance offered to help humans secure it.

Cotton Mather, when commenting on the Joseph passage in his *Biblia Americana,* noted that there was a *"Republican Strain"* running through the Bible's *"Way of Governing."* The tragedy evident in the story of Joseph was that *"Eleutherians,"* a word he coined for "Friends of *Liberty,"* are forced to see a biblical hero *"enslaving a Free People"* in order to ingratiate himself to a monarch. Cotton wrote that he resisted the notion of condemning Joseph, but in the end he had to agree that *"Joseph,* tho' a good Man, enslaved a *Free-born People,* and introduced Arbitrary Power into *Egypt,* with all its terrible Consequences."

When Cotton looked in the Bible for a godly constitutional structure, he did not find it laid out in one passage; rather, he pieced it together from many hints and indications. Commenting in the *Biblia Americana* on the passage where Moses' father-in-law recommended the creation of a hierarchical system of judges, Mather offered his readers his own most complete description of what seemed to him to be "Jewish polity," or what previous Dutch writers had called "the Hebrew Republic."

The focal point of this constitutional structure is the "chief civil magistrate." This office was held first by Moses, then Joshua, then leading judges, some of whom are named in the Book of Judges and 1 Samuel, then eventually the monarchs of Israel. By this structure, Israel was what the British called a "limited monarchy" or "constitutional monarchy." This chief civil magistrate did not, however, have absolute power. God was the true "high king" and Cotton agreed with Josephus

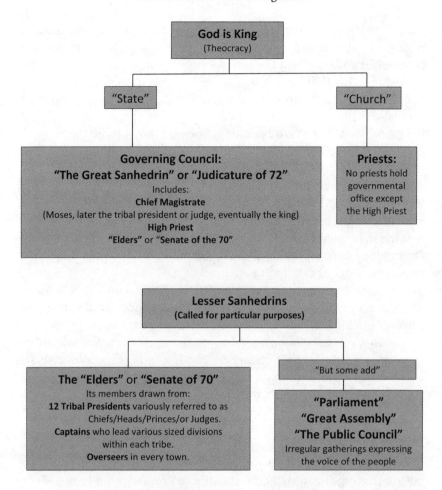

Cotton Mather's Hebrew Republic. As with many other scholars of the Reformation and Protestant Enlightenment, Cotton interpreted passages in the Old Testament, especially Exodus 18–19, Joshua 23–24, and 1 Samuel 8, as indicating that the Jews were generally organized in a republican fashion with a mixed government, separation of church and state, a representative system in a senate, and a venue for the people to express their will. Cotton Mather believed that there was a "republican strain" in the Bible that encouraged all state and religious institutions to be organized to facilitate widespread representation and to promote the people's freedom. Cotton supported the Glorious Revolution of 1688 because he believed that King James II and Governor Edmund Andros in New England were making themselves tyrants in that they undermined the republican ideals of God and England.

that this truth made it correct to call the system a "theocracy." On the other hand, most decision making was handled by a governing council. At times, the people might have a direct role in government. In the classical language of republicanism, Israel had a structure that affirmed separation of church and state along with decentralization of power. A wit in England called this political tradition "Talmudical commonwealthmen" — the commonwealthmen in England being the political theorists who greatly influenced John Adams, James Madison, Thomas Jefferson, and others who are considered founding fathers of the political tradition of the United States.

The "republican strain" of thought that Cotton found in the Bible entailed even deeper notions than just models for limited monarchy and a government founded upon the consent of the governed. The most important of all political ideas for Cotton Mather was the *eleutherian* theme running throughout the Bible and early church. In the New Testament the Greek word for freedom is *eleutheria,* and the offer of freedom, both earthly and heavenly, is central to the message of the various books of the New Testament. Jesus offers his followers freedom, and Paul, in one of his most ringing passages, declares to the Galatians: "It is for freedom that Christ has set us free!" (5:1).

Cotton Mather merged the tradition of Talmudical commonwealthmen with a distinctly Anglo-Protestant tradition he called *eleutherian.* He wrote most directly about this tradition in his *Eleutheria* of 1698, but used the term throughout his life in other publications. *Eleutheria* was a history of Protestant freedom in Britain. Like all British schoolchildren, Cotton had learned an entangled political and religious tradition that reached back through medieval books such as Monmouth's *History of the Kings of Britain* to Bede's *Ecclesiastical History of the English People.* This long tradition asserted that England had been first civilized by freedmen who had been enslaved in Greece from the Trojan War. Roman republican principles had been installed in Britain around the time of Christ planting the seeds for the fullness of Christian freedom. They were established in England by King Lucius, who learned the faith from the appropriately named Bishop Eleutherius of Rome. All this happened long before the rise of authoritarian regimes, both political and Christian, in imperial Rome. The moral of this history was that the foundation of British politics and Christian churches was the fellowship of free people.

Cotton Mather found this republican tradition in both the Old and

New Testaments of the Bible and in the history of Great Britain. Sadly, he also found various stories in each of these sources of how authoritarian powers had often conspired to undermine the people's freedom and how the people themselves, in their fickleness and sin, often preferred slavery to freedom. Just as Lot's wife turned to look back on Sodom and the Hebrew people in the desert looked back longingly to Egypt, the people of Britain always needed leaders to rise up among them to remind them of, and lead them toward, the fullness of freedom in Christ.

In his commentary on Joshua, Cotton placed himself among the *eleutherians* — those who pursued the fullness of political and religious liberty and were horrified by the way Joseph "seems to have destroyed the freedom of the nation, and to have committed a horrid rape on their liberties and properties" in order "to ingratiate himself with his monarch." When Cotton joined the insurgency against the royal government's representative in New England, he joined as the opposite of a Joseph figure. He would not encourage the tyranny of a governor or a king. He would fight alongside other leading "gentlemen" who were all justified in their revolutionary actions by traditions of British and biblical republicanism.

The Protestant Interest

With the downfall of the royal governor came the rule of a semi-official provisional government in Boston. Nobody did anything radical. Increase Mather, being in London already, was perfectly situated to represent the new colonial government to William and Mary, the king and queen brought to power by the Glorious Revolution. Cotton Mather and the other ministers of Boston returned to their churches but were anxious to find a way that would encourage peace and stability. Cotton also continued as an advisor and useful pen within the government.

Former governor Simon Bradstreet, eighty-six years old, took control of the provisional government. He had been the governor of Massachusetts from 1679 to 1684 and was experienced with imperial politics. The people of New England revered him as a wise and good Puritan magistrate. To fill out the provisional government, Bradstreet gathered around him men with good reputations for both piety and public service. One of the key advisors to Bradstreet was William Stoughton. He was in his middle fifties and had been very effective as a stabilizing force in the April revolution. Highly respected for his piety, when he was young Stoughton had several times been sought by Cotton Mather's grandfather to share his pastorate in Dorchester. But Stoughton did not feel the call. He eventually became a well-travelled, long-term bachelor — both a rarity in Massachusetts. He also became active in law and politics, well known as a moderate and pragmatic voice with a heart set on the best interest of Massachusetts. Politicians often received land as payment for services, and Stoughton had managed his land and investments well. He was rich, well read, and enjoyed being a philanthropist and benefactor to good causes and institutions. Surprising to many back when the charter was initially lost, Stoughton had served honorably and well under the hated royal governor. Later, when Stoughton stood with the leaders of the April revolution, it helped make people like Cotton Mather feel confident that the colonists were not overreacting. As a reward for his steadfast loyalty to high principles on both sides of the political fence, the new king soon designated Stoughton as "Lieutenant Governor" and retained him as chief justice of the courts in Massachusetts. Bradstreet and Stoughton held Massachusetts together well for three years by managing through consensus. Moderation was the key as they waited for news from England about the colony's future.

The geopolitical map of the Atlantic world had radically changed in the late 1680s. The major players on that map — the British, French, Spanish, and Indian — were contesting for control of the Atlantic coast of North America. Religion mixed with politics as Protestants in Britain and Europe needed to unify in the face of the Roman Catholic threat from France and Spain. Missionary activity among the Indians needed to increase, not just because it was the Christian thing to do, but also because it was the strategic political thing to do. The Roman Catholics had a cadre of effective missionaries converting Indians into allies of the French and Spanish. Protestantism also needed to have Indian allies.

In his book *The Protestant Interest: New England after Puritanism,* Thomas Kidd describes how Protestants of the era felt "beleaguered." They sensed they were losing the great spiritual and geopolitical battle for the gospel. "The Protestant interest" became a catch phrase of the era for a renewed sense of purpose for a more unified Protestantism within the British Empire. Cotton Mather used the phrase. For him the new Protestant monarchy of William and Mary secured the British Empire for the Protestant cause. Cotton was a young man looking forward.

He would write the history of New England's isolated Puritan past, but he would fight for the expansive goals of the new Protestant interest. If Protestantism was to survive in North America, the ministers needed to support the empire.

Perry Miller, one of the best interpreters of New England thought, described Cotton Mather as an exemplar of an "Augustinian strain of piety," the form of piety that emphasizes the sovereignty of God and sinfulness of humanity. It is appropriate to add that Cotton's life and thought also exemplified an Augustinian strain of entanglement. St. Augustine was a great muddier of waters and a proponent of lowered expectations. In his *City of God,* Augustine emphasized that Christians live in a secular age in which the heavenly realm of God and the earthly realm of humanity are "entangled together and intermixed." Augustine encouraged Christians to live piously and pursue spiritual purity, but at the same time he advised Christians to lower their expectations of church and state. Purity was only to be found in heaven. Christians should expect to get messy in their messy world.

In the Glorious Revolution and its aftermath, Cotton got messy. During these years he realized that the purity hoped for and indicated in the name "Puritan" would never be attained in either the colony's politics or its religion. His grandparents and parents had hoped to create a City on a Hill, a model republic, far from England, where purified churches would be the foundation of politics. But that colony was now a province and no longer isolated from imperial politics and imperial religion. Compromises must be made and expectations lowered. While Cotton was learning this in America, his father was learning it in England. The "republican strain" in the Bible had to be modified to support the empire's constitutional monarchy. Gospel freedom, the freedom in Christ, needed to be distinguished from republican freedom and British citizenship. After the heady first days of the April revolution, practical realities sobered any thoughts of perfecting a godly republic. Such sober thoughts did not mean that Cotton would stop calling people to holiness. In Augustinian fashion Cotton strove all the more to call the people of New England to holiness — no one could rest until he or she rested in God — but the call to holiness needed to be more personal and less associated with institutions of church and state.

Such was the context for a dinner party at Samuel Sewall's house on February 24, 1690. Sewall and his wife, Hannah, fitted out a long table in their great room for the dinner. Invited were seventeen people, including Governor and Lady Bradstreet; Lieutenant Governor Stoughton; Major Thomas Hutchinson and wife; Mr. Thomas Brattle; Sewall's pastor at South Church, Mr. Samuel Willard; and Maria Mather accompanied by her son Cotton. On the face of it, the dinner was an opportunity to talk about Sewall's recent experiences in England where he had gone on many sightseeing trips with Increase Mather and Thomas Brattle. That week Cotton had turned twenty-seven years old. He greatly respected the men and women around the table. They were all model citizens of church and state. If the old Puritan vision of a self-governed City on a Hill was gone, these people at this table were rightfully at the center of re-envisioning a new role for New England within the British Empire.

As for the dinner, Sewall noted in his diary that everybody fit well at the table. Cotton Mather "returned thanks in an excellent manner" and ended the prayer by leading the table in singing Psalm 56. Cotton, who was an expert at translating Hebrew psalms into meters appropriate for easy singing, supplied the words, and Sewall, often song leader in his church, set the tune. We can take a moment to imagine the scene: a long table, candlelight flickering on the guests' faces, all united in a song before the serving of a lavish dinner. The writer of Psalm 56, though beset with fears, says he will trust in God no matter what. He fears that malicious enemies band together and lie in wait, but "I have bound myself with vows made to you, God, and will redeem them with due thank-offerings."

The choice of the psalm was not without purpose — at some point that evening they would have to discuss the devastating news that had come earlier in the day to Governor Bradstreet: Combined French and Indian forces had massacred British colonists at Schenectady near Albany, New York. After dinner, as the Sewalls had been warned, there would be more guests arriving as Governor Bradstreet needed to be counseled as to proper action.

So with dinner over, the plates were cleared. Chairs from around the house were brought down to the great hall. More glasses were brought to the table along with more of the sweet Madeira wine from the Portuguese Islands. Arriving as if on cue were others from the inner circle of the provisional government: Mr. Thomas Danforth, Major John Richards, Major General Wait Still Winthrop, Col. Samuel Shrimpton, and Mr. Isaac Addington. The highest levels of military and political leadership were now gathered around the Sewall table to discuss the danger of French and Indian invasion into Massachusetts from both the east and the north. A militia needed to be mustered immediately, but the big picture required renewed missionary work among the Indians. The Indians held the balance of power in New England, and their loyalties to either the French or the British varied from place to place and person to person. All at the table agreed to fully support what was called "the New England Company," a missionary organization the formal name for which was "the Company for the Propagation of the Gospel in New England and parts adjacent in America."

Samuel Sewall and Cotton Mather both served throughout their adult lives as "commissioners" for the New England Company. The company existed in London and its members were conscientious men of wealth and prestige. The money that they collected was allotted to commissioners in New England for distribution to support evangelism. The commissioners disbursed stipends to ministers, paid for the translation and publication of Bibles, sermons, tracts, and textbooks, and helped fund the building of meetinghouses and schools in Indian praying towns. Sewall and Cotton were both dedicated to the success of this organization, and over the next thirty years no one would do more than Cotton Mather in keeping it vigorous.

Cotton Mather's role in geopolitics was evangelistic. Cotton, like most evangelists and missionaries in history, believed that the gospel would empower all who embraced it, but also, as is often the case, he had a rather naïve sense that the gospel would serve the political, cultural, and earthly hopes of the country supporting the evangelism. Cotton believed that the gospel empowered Indians in a way that would also serve to justify and support the Protestant interest of the British Empire. Like John Eliot, the revered Apostle to the Indians, Cotton promoted preaching to the Indians, organizing Indian praying towns, offering British-style educational opportunities up to and including the opportunity to go to Harvard College, teaching them logic, rhetoric, and multiple dead and living languages, encouraging them to marry and raise families, and most importantly inspiring them with the duty to spread the gospel themselves among other Indians further into the interior of America — all this Cotton assumed would in the end serve both the heavenly kingdom and the earthly British Empire.

In the short run of colonial Massachusetts, it is not clear how much Cotton's politically entangled heart for Indian evangelism helped the British ward off French encroachment. However, over the course of the following century, there were many Indians who fought on the side of the British. As for the ultimate evangelistic success of the New England Company, many Indians did become and remain Protestants. However, David Silverman in *Red Brethren* writes of the Indian efforts to disentangle their Christianity from British and American culture. Eventually, he writes, "by proselytizing each other, worshipping together, and supporting each other as they took charge of their own congregations and communities," the Indians were able to free themselves from the myopia of the Protestant interest. Cotton Mather, on the other hand, was never completely able to disentangle his missionary work among Indians from his deep commitment to British culture.

The Devil in Salem

With the shipwreck of charters, the arrival of a royal governor bent on undermining both freedom and the rights of private property, the subsequent one-day revolution, the uncertainty of what the new charter would entail, and the rising fear of French and Indian invasions, many New England towns and churches were contorted with stress between 1686 and 1692. None was more contorted than Salem Village, a hamlet near Salem that Satan used for the purpose of dragging the whole colony into a fiasco of mismanagement that has ever after smeared the reputation of Puritanism.

Witchcraft was afoot in the village. It was both a sin and a civil offense, so as the situation spun into proportions beyond the borders of the village, both ministers and magistrates from throughout the colony got involved. If the situation had been left to the regional ministers, all would have probably worked out to some level of common satisfaction; however, the magistrates bungled their role. Upon hearing of the witchcraft in Salem Village and demon possession of girls, Cotton Mather recommended the kind of healing program that had worked four years earlier with the Goodwin children in Boston. The girls, he recommended, should be dispersed to live for a while in calm and healthy homes where good women — commonsensical women like his wife, Abigail — would watch their diet, make sure they had plenty of sleep, and guide them through daily chores. With the girls' lives being thus regulated, family, friends, and ministers should join together in long sessions of prayer. If Cotton's advice had been followed, it is safe to assume that matters in Salem would have turned out better.

The civil offense of practicing witchcraft was a matter for the judiciary, and, as the proportions of the situation grew, a special ad-hoc court was formed to handle the situation. William Stoughton, John Richards, and Samuel Sewall were commissioned as judges to restore order by proper jurisprudence and appropriate punishment. However, order was not attained. The witch trials turned into a chaotic mixture of pseudo-scientific notions, social dysfunction, misuse of inadequate laws of evidence, and overly quick executions. William Stoughton, chief judge of the trials, failed in his duty to create a trustworthy court. The executions of witches were unsettling, and afterwards there was no sense of closure or justice. Samuel Sewall later declared to his church that he was willing "to take the blame and shame" of the trials upon himself. In his history of New England, Cotton agreed that the executions proceeded from mistaken principles. After it was all over, nineteen people had been executed and almost everyone involved believed that the Devil had worked his mischief and come out on top.

Over the course of the following three centuries, Cotton Mather became the name most associated with the witch trials, but Cotton never attended the trials nor did he have any authority within the situation. He did preach at one of the executions and did gather with other ministers to try to advise the judges to be more moderate and careful with the evidence, but, overall, his participation was peripheral.

There is, however, one minor matter in the context of the witch trials that is important for understanding Cotton Mather's role in the beginnings of the American evangelical tradition: the difference between him and Thomas Brattle as seen in letters that both wrote concerning the witch trials. Cotton was twenty-nine and Brattle thirty-four. Both considered themselves leading scholars within the intellectual elite of New England, and each wrote a letter hoping to influence the intellectual quality of the jurisprudence being applied in Salem. The difference between the two letters exposes a rift between rationalism and reasonableness that would harden in the following years. After the witch trials, Thomas Brattle became one of the principal members of a party pressing for a more genteel imperial Protestantism that shunned the irrationalism of eccentric belief in witches, demons, angels, and natural impossibilities. Cotton Mather, on the other hand, found himself the leader of a populist perspective he called "the evangelical interest" that promoted the reasonableness of these beliefs and others when appropriately affirmed by credible sources and properly regulated by biblical models. Thomas Brattle and Cotton Mather seem to have long been happy to ignore each other; however, after 1692 the deep division between the two spun out into a deep division between religious rationalism and biblical enlightenment. The difference between the two letters is early evidence of an intellectual rift with long implications for the American evangelical tradition.

Cotton Mather wrote his letter on May 31, a few days before Stoughton called into session the most famous of the witch trial courts. Cotton wrote specifically to Judge John Richards, who was one of his parishioners, but he expected all the judges to read the letter. The core of Thomas Brattle's letter was written in August after the third set of executions. An expanded version of the letter appeared on October 8. On the whole, Cotton Mather and Thomas Brattle agreed with each other on jurisprudential issues. Both letters advise the judges of problems concerning the use of apparitions and alleged statements by apparitions as evidence. Both Mather and Brattle agreed that such evidence, even if accepted in the court, should not be the sole basis for a conviction.

Despite their agreement about jurisprudence, the assumptions within the letters differ radically. Thomas Brattle was intensely interested in reasoning based on the model of mathematics. There is no evidence for assuming that his interest in mathematics undermined his Christianity. In fact, Brattle had recently returned from England where he had met Robert Boyle, a famous advocate for a positive relationship between the new science and Christian orthodoxy. Brattle seems to have even modeled his own life after the revered bachelor and "Christian Virtuoso."

On the other hand, there is a restrictive and overly mathematical tone in Brattle's rationalism that came out in his letter about the witch trials. The October 8 version of the letter begins by declaring that a proper understanding of Cartesian mechanical philosophy will expose errors in assumptions being used by the judges about the relationship between matter and spirit. The judges, Brattle pointed out, assumed that "venomous and malignant particles" can be ejected at will from the eye of a witch that could cause fits and convulsions in the girls. Brattle, contradicting the judges, insisted that mechanical philosophy does not allow for a person to control such emissions from the eye. "The reasonable part of the world," Brattle asserted, will laugh at the judges' "ignorance and folly."

This is both harsh and boxy in its thinking. Throughout the letter Brattle used logic in this way to distinguish black from white and leave no grey possibilities in the middle. The reader is not encouraged to think in terms of entanglements of matter and spirit; rather, there are only rather stupid people and the obviously smart. He several times called the judges "superstitious" because they believed reports involving spiritual agency in the world. At one point he declared, tongue-in-cheek, that it "may be mathematically demonstrated to any man of common sense" that the judges were taking testimony from the Devil when they took the testimony of a person who reported what the Devil told him. Brattle's logic is not inappropriate in a letter on jurisprudence; however, his stark use of logic to distinguish the superstitious from the rational leaves little room for humility in the face of spiritual mysteries and jurisprudential quandaries involving reports of witchcraft. At the end of the letter Brattle baldly stated: "Furthermore: These afflicted persons do say, and often have declared it, that they can see specters when their eyes are shut. . . . I am sure they lie, at least speak falsely, . . . for the thing, in nature, is an utter impossibility."

For Cotton Mather, it was not reasonable to be so confident. The word "impossible" was not useful when approaching the Bible or events in which spiritual beings were involved. Cotton never allowed himself to be trapped by logic when trying to understand the Bible or the complexities of God's creations. The Bible led Cotton to believe that the cosmos was wild with both natural laws and miracles. Jesus physically passed through walls in the New Testament. Why should eyelids necessarily inhibit sight? The material world is complicated. Angels physically "troubled the water" at the Pool of Bethesda — the incident in the Bible for which Cotton named his medical book. Cotton believed the relationship between spirit and matter was not black and white. Therefore, it was not reasonable for Brattle to declare the afflicted girls to be "liars" because of his own Cartesian assumptions about the limits of matter and spirit. Cotton was a pastor with a pastor's ability to empathize and open up to truths spoken even by young girls. The girls needed to be treated with respect, and their accounts of what was going on listened to with ears to hear. Cotton did not believe that witches should be executed on the basis of what the girls said they saw; however, that did not mean the experiences of the girls should be discounted as lies or obviously false statements. Both God and Satan often were active in the experiences of children.

Unlike Brattle's letter, Cotton Mather's letter to the witch trial judges was respectful and reasonable. Brattle's letter assumed that "superstition" was afoot when witchcraft was legally recognized to be a not-uncommon activity among those antagonistic to Christianity. Brattle's letter was more interested in logical fallacies than jurisprudence. Cotton's letter worked with the legal definition of a witch: a person who "having free use of reason" seeks and obtains from "the Devil, or any other god, besides the true God Jehovah, an ability to do strange things, or things which he cannot by his own abilities arrive unto." By this definition the key to finding a witch is finding evidence of a person's "free use of reason." Cotton wrote in his letter that evidence from the afflicted girls about what they saw or heard involving apparitions was very weak evidence for what was actually going on in the minds of the accused witches. Evidence for conviction needed to come from the witches themselves in the form of clear and direct confession. Without extremely strong evidence, Cotton, like his father and many other ministers, thought that it was better to be lenient than too strict.

These two letters, arising as they do at the beginning of post-Puritan New England, expose a rift between those who followed the Bible into a world of wild wonders and those who followed the rationalizing and simplifying tendencies of the Reformation into a world less complex and less wild. Many scholars, looking back on the decade of the 1690s, see the slide into the genteel Protestantism of the empire as a process of "secularization." Charles Taylor in his book *The Secular Age* writes that the slide "was not the result of 'reason' and 'science,' but reflected a deep-seated moral distaste for the old religion that sees God as an agent in history." Brattle's letter exemplifies this distaste along with Taylor's following point that it became easy to write-off Bible-based thinking about God's agency as "pandering to popular fears and illusions, offering an utterly unworthy picture of God." Both Brattle and Mather were orthodox Protestants; however, Brattle was worried about gullibility, about superstition, about believing too much. For Brattle, spirit and matter were governed by rational laws. Mather, on the other hand, was more worried about believing too little than believing too much. For him as for Isaiah, God's thoughts are not human thoughts, and God's ways are not human ways.

The Levitation of Margaret Rule

Cotton Mather believed that during the period of the late 1680s and throughout the 1690s the old Puritan commonwealths of New England were a spiritual battlefield. Evil angels, minions of Satan, targeted individual towns, churches, and people of particular weakness. Thankfully, good angels, hosts of heaven, were sent to help the weak against the forces of evil. Since Cotton was a collector of remarkable providences, he early on began to discern the heightened intensity of the battle for New England. Pastors sent stories to him of spiritual events in their congregations, and he would transcribe them and circulate them among other pastors. There was a lively network of shared information among pastors that Cotton helped facilitate. Cotton himself contributed to the network by reporting on remarkable providences happening in Boston and at sea. On his walks along the North End wharfs Cotton heard of many remarkable providences. Sifting the stories to separate the incredible from the credible was a common activity for him. Credibility was a matter of trustworthy sources. Incredibility was the stuff of untrustworthy sources.

One of the most remarkable of providences that Cotton circulated among New England pastors happened in his own congregation. Satan had targeted two girls within his own North Church; however, grace abounding, the attack was turned into a youth revival, an "awakening" as he called it. An attack by Satan was dramatically confronted and the youth in his church were the winners. Wounded in the battle was Cotton's reputation among those who wanted to believe the worst about him. By standing with his congregation, he allowed himself to become a target.

Five years earlier, four years before the witch trials in Salem, Cotton and Abigail Mather had taken in the demon-possessed Martha Goodwin and had helped heal the thirteen-year-old girl with a regimen of prayer, diet, sleep, and household chores. Cotton was not some sort of "faith-healer" or miracle worker. He thought of himself as a physician with a holistic view of health. Sick people needed first and foremost to be embraced within a fellowship of love and mutual responsibility. Demon possession was healed best by a community at prayer followed by good diet, good sleep, good friends, and good exercise.

Four years later, around the same time that the girls in Salem were being made into a public spectacle, a similarly troubled teenage woman appeared in the North End of Boston needing to be healed. Her name was Mercy Short. She was seventeen years old and had experienced the horror of Indian attack and captivity. Her freedom had been purchased from the Indians, but she was returned an orphan. Cotton and

Top: North Church meetinghouse on the triangular North Square — a center of wealth and respectability that was also at the center of New England's "evangelical" party. Cotton Mather preached to 1500 people in North Church's meetinghouse. The meetinghouse, rebuilt after a fire in 1676, was designed in the four-square style under a hipped roof with enlarged dormers to bring in more light. North Church meetinghouse was similar to the Hingham meetinghouse (bottom) constructed five years later in 1681. (Detail from William Burgis's map of Boston drawn in 1728. Map reproduction courtesy of the Norman B. Leventhal Map Center at the Boston Public Library. The drawing of Hingham meetinghouse is by Marty Saunders and used with her permission. See Peter Benes's *Meetinghouses of Early New England*, pp. 92-101.)

Abigail reached out to her, and she apparently moved into the Mather house. Cotton wrote of the "spectral outcries" coming from his house to which his neighbors had to listen. Mercy claimed to be bewitched by Sarah Good, one of the condemned witches from the Salem trials. Mercy stayed in the North End and the North Church offered her prayer and fellowship while she also went through Cotton and Abigail's regimen. As with the case of Martha Goodwin, Cotton did not take credit for healing Mercy Short. While under the care of the North Church and participating in the meetings organized for youth, Mercy was healed most directly by an angel dressed in "white glittering robes" who appeared to her.

Once healed, Mercy was welcomed fully into the life of the North Church. It may be that, given Cotton's concern for orphans, Mercy continued to live with the Mather family. A little over a year later, Mercy was admitted into full communion in North Church after having testified to the saving work of Christ in her life. Being seventeen, she participated in North Church youth fellowship-groups. Another of the teenage women in these groups was Margaret Rule, who herself became intermittently possessed by demons between September and the end of October, 1693. As her pastors, Cotton and his father took the lead in organizing her healing. Unlike Martha Goodwin and Mercy Short, Margaret already had a home in the neighborhood, so she did not move in with Abigail and Cotton. She remained in her parents' home. As with the healing of Martha and Mercy, Margaret's healing was a community endeavor. Cotton mentions "standers by" watching and listening during his interviews with Margaret. As with Mercy, Margaret was eventually healed by an angel, apparently the same angel that Mercy had seen. Cotton did not see an angel either time, but he had no reason to disbelieve the testimony of the teenage women.

Before being healed, Margaret was dramatically levitated by demons. Cotton Mather was not present at Margaret's levitation. But credible North End neighbors were there in her room when "her tormenters pulled her up to the ceiling of the chamber and held her there before a very numerous company of spectators, who found it as much as they could all do to pull her down again." We know about this because Cotton later listed it among several wonders in a report of this and other aspects of Margaret's possession that he sent out in manuscript to be circulated among New England ministers. Matters got out of hand when a highly critical Bostonian named Robert Calef, a merchant who shared

Thomas Brattle's critical spirit and insistent rationalism, got hold of Mather's account and turned the incident, along with the whole Margaret Rule story, into a transatlantic kerfuffle. Calef hated Cotton Mather and eventually published in London a highly partisan and unsupported collection of letters earlier written in Boston that has long served as fodder for those who want to believe the worst about Cotton Mather.

Calef, like Brattle, was quick to label the testimony of eyewitnesses "impossible." Levitation by demons was absurd in Calef's view. In his letters he held Cotton up for ridicule and called upon Cotton to defend himself. Mather eventually responded, emphasizing that many credible witnesses were present at every important aspect of the Margaret Rule story. Cotton supplied Calef with three letters containing the attestation of six credible eyewitnesses affirming their presence at the levitation.

Calef offered no contrary evidence, only scorn. Historians have never been able to learn much about who Calef was, but Cotton noted that he was "offended" by the witch trials and by Cotton's earlier book about the healing of the Goodwin children. Calef called all Mather's accounts of various demon possessions "incredible romances." For over a decade, Calef, apparently encouraged by others in Boston, kept ratcheting up his antagonism until he finally published a book ridiculing Cotton in London. Worse than attacking Cotton for believing in levitation, Calef went further, implying that Cotton's involvement with the girls was more sexual than spiritual. Across the Atlantic, far from anyone actually involved in the story, Calef published an anonymous letter that he said he transcribed, a letter that purported to describe a day when both Increase and Cotton Mather visited Margaret Rule. The letter says she was lying in bed and the two Mathers sat beside the bed. The letter further says that thirty to forty persons, including young men and women, were in the room watching as Cotton and Increase asked the girl a barrage of odd questions. Several times, the letter states, Cotton rubbed the seventeen-year-old's bare breasts.

Cotton denied the account and no one ever came forward to corroborate it. But it was published in London, and Cotton mourned for his reputation. He could accept ridicule for believing the solid testimony of North Enders about Margaret Rule's levitation; however, the publication of an anonymous and "smutty" letter designed to undermine the moral integrity of his and his father's ministry cut him deeply. He could never defend himself among those in London who wanted to believe the worst, but happily, his reputation was secure with his neighbors and congregation — the people who were supposed to have watched him do the deed. Cotton and Abigail's home continued to be the center of a hectic daily ministry that only got more chaotic as revival broke out in the neighborhood.

The experience of the two young women, Mercy and Margaret, "awakened" many of their peers who belonged to the private prayer meetings that Cotton had organized for young people of both sexes. The teenagers of the North End were not insensitive to two of their own being possessed and dramatically healed. During Margaret's possession a young people's prayer group organized themselves into a constant, twenty-four-hour prayer cycle lasting for a week. The teens sang psalms together and offered devotions. "Scores of other young people, who were strangers to real piety," were joining together in private prayer meetings, having been affected by the "demonstrations of Hell" that they had witnessed when visiting the possessed young women. "Behold," Cotton declared — behold the results of demonic attacks in the neighborhood and slanderous libels — "the Devil got just nothing; but God got praises, Christ got subjects, the Holy Spirit got temples, the Church got additions, and the souls of men got everlasting benefits." All things were working together for the good.

American Historian and Boston Ebenezer

Cotton was thirty and Abigail twenty-four when the angel healed Margaret Rule. That year Abigail gave birth to a baby boy that lived less than a week. The Mathers continued to have only one living child, seven-year-old Katherine or "Katy." That year she became dangerously sick and Cotton thought she was going to die. Resigned to her fate, Cotton took up a Bible. Upon opening it, his eye fell on "the story of our Lord's raising the little daughter of the ruler of the synagogue in the eighth chapter of Luke." Cotton, who considered himself the equivalent of a synagogue ruler, wrote that he read it with tears, then his tears turned to prayers. He begged for the life of his child. Immediately Katy "fell into a critical and plentiful bleeding and recovered that hour."

The following June, Abigail gave birth to the only one of her children who would live to marry and give Cotton grandchildren. This girl was also named Abigail, often called "Nibby." Another daughter, Hannah or "Nanny," came two years later. Hannah would be the only one of

Abigail's nine children to outlive Cotton. In 1699 Abigail gave birth to a son named Increase or "Cresy." In the 1690s Cotton embraced being a family man. Cotton had begun the decade believing that God had called him to the vocation of pastor, whole-person healer, and family man, and by the end of the decade he was flourishing in all three.

But there also was a fourth vocation he heartily desired to succeed at. He wanted to be a historian. Of all his scholarly interests, he was most intent upon being known throughout the Republic of Letters as a wise and discerning historian. His first work of history in which he claimed the title historian was his journalistic account of the 1688 possession of the Goodwin children. Its publication in London encouraged his hope for scholarly success. His next most important work of history, the first in which he attempted to show the long-term development of a political and religious idea, was his *Eleutheria: or, An Idea of the Reformation in England and A History of Non-Conformity in and since that Reformation.* That work offered a historical framework for his deepest beliefs about the purpose of church and state, and the ongoing need for British Christians to aspire to that purpose. Cotton's role as spokesman for freedom and consent of the governed in the Massachusetts revolution of 1689 can only be understood in the light of this history that he wrote afterwards.

It was soon after the chaotic events of 1692-93 that Cotton settled into the work that would, in the long run, make him the greatest *American* historian of the seventeenth and eighteenth centuries. He started collecting, organizing, and drafting two massive works: the *Biblia Americana* and the *Magnalia Christi Americana.* In the former Cotton analyzes, among other things, the biblical narrative of history up through the book of Acts, then beyond Acts into the history of Jewish, Islamic, and Christian politics on three continents up through the beginning of the seventeenth century. The latter part of the *Biblia Americana* is focused on the history of religious toleration and religious freedom for Jews. That work, which he added to throughout the rest of his life, became too unwieldy for publication. Only now, over three hundred years later, is it being fully published. While working on that larger project, Cotton also worked on steadily collecting, editing, and writing a religious and political history of New England called *Magnalia Christi Americana,* the "Great American Deeds of Christ." In 1698 it was finished and in 1702 it was published in London. With its publication, Cotton became an internationally known historian.

73

The *Magnalia* is a monument to the entangled values of church and state during the seventeenth century. It looks backwards to the founding of Puritan republics in New England while also journalistically promoting the values of post-Puritan unity and geopolitical mission. At times readers of the *Magnalia* have taken the book too seriously and have said that Cotton wanted to write something like Virgil's *Aeneid.* They get this from the epic tone of the introduction, which begins with "I write of the wonders of the Christian religion flying from the depravations of Europe to the American strand." The *Magnalia,* however, is not designed to offer a grand narrative of American history or destiny. It is actually a massive but humble collection of disparate biographies, narratives, and analyses of various colonial missions, wars, and institutions. Cotton Mather enjoyed thinking of himself as a historian, and he was, in fact, the greatest *American* historian of the colonial era. But it is important not to overburden Cotton with a definition of historian that he did not use. Cotton considered a historian to be a rather middling-sort of scholar, more a scribal figure than high thinker. Historians, according to the classical imagery he appreciated, were like bees and flower pickers wandering about in literary fields gathering facts, accounts, and opinions. According to European literary genres in the seventeenth century, Cotton's *Magnalia Christi Americana* counts as a massive *anthology* or *florilegia,* both words meaning "flower arrangement." The book, which in its most modern form has more than 1300 pages of small print, is an amazing amassment of all sorts of information about New England's various governments and churches with special emphasis on Indian relations and Harvard College. The book collects together much that Cotton did not write. More scrapbook than monograph, the *Magnalia* has to be read carefully in order to distinguish Cotton's actual words from what he transcribes.

In the *Magnalia* Cotton presents himself as a happy historian. Like Herodotus he sometimes chats with his readers, especially skeptical readers. When introducing a section on military history, Cotton asks: "If the author has taken delight in [writing] this history . . . why should any betray such ill nature as to be angry at it?" Cotton enjoyed writing history. For the most part, he stuck closely to his sources. Some of his biographies are mere eulogies in which he waxes syrupy; however, on the whole the book gathers and assesses eyewitness reports and documents that would have otherwise been lost long ago. Cotton is tenaciously loyal to the legacy of the Puritans and praises the "Congregational church discipline" that the Puritans created in America; however, he is broad-minded too. He criticizes those with "an unhappy narrowness of soul" who are too insistent on their own particular form of Christianity. "Whatever this history be," Cotton tells his readers, "it aims at the doing of good, as well as the telling of truth."

It is important to note that the *Magnalia* does not present American Christianity as better than Europe's, nor does he promote, as others would later do, a belief that America is the new Israel to which Christ will return. Cotton considered his account of Christ's great American deeds to be only a small part of a larger "Christianography" — the writing of the great deeds of Christ in the progress toward global Christianity. Cotton was excited by the missional opportunities of the revived British Empire under William and Mary. European Protestantism in the seventeenth century was only beginning to respond to the Great Commission by sending missionaries out into the world. Anticipating the popular evangelical missionary biographies of the nineteenth century, and fifty years before the publication of Jonathan Edwards's popular *Life of David Brainerd,* Cotton included in the *Magnalia* his widely popular biography of John Eliot, the "Apostle to the Indians." Cotton Mather revered John Eliot because of his lifelong dedication to the hard work of evangelism, especially the scholarly work of learning native languages and translating the Bible.

New England's greatest frustration, as presented in the *Magnalia,* was the colony's failure to achieve permanent and widespread unity with the Indians. Everybody was at fault, but he raged most against the Indians who refused to embrace the British. Cotton transcribed first-hand accounts of women and children being kidnapped by Indians and told many stories of frontier atrocities. Some of the most ugly things Cotton ever wrote were voiced out of his fear that Indians held the key to the downfall or progress of everything good and British in America. He was able to write about the early Pequot wars and the devastating King Philip's war of his youth with a bit of rhetorical distance. However, the renewed wars of the 1690s cut him deeply. The French and Indians were bearing down on New England as he was writing the *Magnalia* even as the other British colonies in America were at peace. "Is it not a very humbling thing," he asked his readers, that Governor Andros, the man whom he had helped depose, had created an Indian peace for all the British colonies in America, but "poor New England" is "the only land still embroiled in war?" Mather prays: "thou has humbled us, and shown us great and sore troubles, and brought us down into the depths of the earth." The last line of the *Magnalia* quotes Lamentations: "Let us search and try our ways, and turn again unto the Lord."

Even with this last line, the *Magnalia* is an optimistic book overall. Given the political and religious upheavals of the 1680s and 90s along with the simple fact that the Puritans had lost their charter, and with it independent control of the colony, a reader might expect the whole book to be one long lament. If his father, Increase, had written it, the book probably would have been more of a rant against declining Puritan piety. The *Magnalia,* however, is full of hope about the new government and the new, more tolerant, religious unity available to New England. In the *Magnalia* the future is bright.

Nowhere is this more clear in the *Magnalia* than in Cotton's declaration that Boston has its own guardian angel assigned to it by God. Cotton shared in the deep European and Christian tradition that human fulfillment on earth was most available in happy town life. Puritans in New England believed that God had a special role for towns as the essential structure of colonial politics, church orthodoxy, and liberal arts education. Citing Scripture and early Christian belief, Cotton declared that "there is abundant cause to think that every town in which the Lord Jesus Christ is worshipped, hath an angel to watch over it." Boston, he believed, had its own guardian angel. The best evidence for this was the fact that when a French fleet was on its way to attack Boston harbor, sickness among the sailors had forced the fleet to turn around. "Is it not likely," Cotton asked, "that the angel of the Lord went out to smite the fleet of the Assyrians [French] with a sickness, which the last summer hindered their invading this town?"

Cotton preached this in a town lecture that was one of the last bits added into the *Magnalia Christi Americana.* The sermon was titled: "The Boston Ebenezer: Some Historical Remarks on the State of Boston . . . for Preserving and Promoting the Good State of That, as well as Any Other Town in the Like Circumstance." Boston, he preached, was now sixty-eight years old and had grown to be "the metropolis of the whole English America." There was no looking back. Boston's role within the British Empire was rising. But with great success comes great responsibility. Mather called for more civic piety. He called upon public officials, ministers, justices, constables, townsmen, schoolmasters, and all others who held civic posts to embrace fully their civic responsibilities. The poor must be taken care of. Widows must be helped. Young people must be raised up in wisdom. "Bawdy-houses" must be routed out. "Drinking-houses" must be regulated. "Equity and charity as well as piety" must be promoted.

For over a decade Boston and all New England had been in a transition. The distinctive Puritan charter for a City on a Hill was gone. New England was now fully integrated into a revived Protestant-British-Atlantic empire. Cotton believed that although Satan was still out and about sowing mischief, God would win in the end. Good angels were guarding Boston and the towns of New England.

CHAPTER 5

The Birth of the American Evangelical Tradition

1698-1707

The Evangelical Interest Tugs at the Protestant Interest

Late in 1699 Cotton Mather was thirty-six years old when, for all to see in the middle of Boston, a new church was gathered, called the Brattle Street Church. It was a church that not only declared itself in favor of compromises with the practices of the Church of England, but also architecturally embraced the favored church-style of the British Empire. To moderate-minded Protestants, there was no cause for alarm. The church practices being advocated were inconsequential and involved such matters as saying the Lord's Prayer and allowing people to become full members without having orally to share their testimony with the whole congregation. Architecturally, the meetinghouse merely incorporated distinctive Anglican features such as a long, single-gabled "English roof," a bell tower with arched openings, and a spire visible to all approaching ships. Cotton declared the church "new indeed!" and its presence in Boston scared him. Thirty years later, when multiple steeples punctuated the Boston skyline, there was still cause for fear. Joseph Sewall, the young pastor of South Church, was likewise scared by deeper meanings in the architecture. After watching the workmen raise the spire over his new meetinghouse, Sewall wrote in the church records his prayer: "O Lord hear! Pardon thy people if they are too ambitious of an outward show, and too much conformed to the vanities of the world. O let us not be high minded, but fear."

Post-Puritan New England was changing rapidly. Boston was booming as an important city within the British Empire. Values were being generated less and less from within New England. More and more her

The Brattle Street meetinghouse with rebuilt steeple. Peter Benes notes that the construction of this meetinghouse in 1699 began the shift of New England church architecture away from regional distinctiveness toward the Protestant church forms favored in the British Empire. The linear "English roof," compass-headed tower, and the spire reflected outwardly the England-oriented changes in liturgy and rules of membership that were promoted by the "innovators." The New North congregation that was formed a few years later in 1714 by a faction from Cotton's Old North imitated the Brattle style. Benes proposes that New North may have built the first steeple in New England while I still favor Brattle Street as the first, but either way, the architecture and motives for each manifested, for Cotton, a lukewarm anglicanization opposed to the hotter evangelical interest. (A detail from William Burgis's *A North East View of the Great Town of Boston*, 1743. Courtesy of American Antiquarian Society)

values were imported from the upscale residents of London. The better-sort of Bostonians aspired for their churches and neighborhoods to imitate the better-sort of churches and neighborhoods of London. All this was fine at one level. Pastors such as Cotton Mather and Joseph Sewall were not antagonistic to cultural changes and both believed wholeheartedly that God had a special role for the British Empire to play in history. Chasing British fashions was not necessarily wrong. In the *Biblia Americana* Cotton advises readers not to worry about transitory customs. Paul in 1 Corinthians 11 makes strict statements about hair length for men and hats for women, but Cotton explains that Paul was most likely speaking about deeper gender issues and not actually prescribing a specific hairstyle or head gear to readers. Cotton took to wearing a periwig even though it upset conservative tastes. Architectural ornament and hairstyle were superficial matters of changing fashion.

So why were Cotton Mather and Joseph Sewall fearful of the new church architecture? They were afraid of the motivation behind the style. What was the ambition? Was the congregation merely trying to conform to the vanities of the world? Was it settling into a lukewarm attitude, a turning away from its first love? Cotton was fearful of what the "undertakers" of the Brattle Street Church were really trying to accomplish.

Similar questions concerning motives applied to Harvard College at the same time. In the middle and late 1690s the leaders of Harvard aspired to attain university status within the empire, construct new buildings with more architectural dignity, and bring a wider range of books and ideas into the curriculum. Cotton worked toward these goals alongside his father, Charles Morton, and former schoolmates Thomas Brattle and John Leverett. The five of them moved back and forth between Boston and Harvard College easily and often with Charlestown and the Charlestown Ferry in between. In the late 1690s these five men were closely linked in promoting ecclesiastical and educational reform, but that does not mean they had the same motivations and ambitions. Increase Mather wanted to fulfill the hopes of the Puritan founders of New England. Brattle and Leverett wanted to embrace the new transatlantic culture. And Cotton? He found a kindred spirit in the elderly Charles Morton. The two of them were trying to negotiate a way of cultural accommodation, intellectual sophistication, and personal holiness that was biblically authorized. We today can recognize their perspective as being evangelical.

At a meeting of the Harvard Corporation in October of 1693, Charles Morton asked, "How may the college be made greater and better?" This kind of question was being asked about many things in post-Puritan New England. At that meeting in Cambridge, Morton, Brattle, and Leverett were charged by Increase and the Corporation to "draw up some proposals for the enlargement of the college by new buildings." Within five years Thomas Brattle successfully designed and oversaw construction of two of the most iconic British imperial-style buildings in all America at that time — a college hall and a church meetinghouse. He seems to have been at the center of what Cotton Mather described as a "party" desirous of what historians call "anglicanization," the desire to break down New England's distinctiveness and fully embrace a generic British culture.

Thomas Brattle's father was a wealthy and successful ship captain comfortable with giving orders, recognizing needs, and meeting those needs with action. Captain Brattle had been one of the principal founders in 1669 of Third (South) Church in Boston. The undertakers of that church weathered religious and political controversy because they had not followed the rules when forming their church. Young Thomas Jr. was a boy when substantial men would gather at his house to discuss the handling of these controversies. He learned how to debate religious matters early. A ship captain's son, Thomas loved mathematics, astronomy, and architecture. When in England he visited the Royal Astronomer in Greenwich and studied the architecture of Christopher Wren — the government's leading mathematician-architect. Brattle was so intent on mathematics and architecture that once, while measuring buildings at the palace in Versailles in France, a guard accosted him as a possible spy. Brattle brought his notebooks back to Boston and wanted to try his hand at being an architect. He wanted very much to help New England become "greater and better." Increase Mather approved the unanimous appointment of Brattle as treasurer of Harvard College, a job with broad responsibilities that included oversight of buildings and grounds. In 1698 Thomas Brattle designed and oversaw the construction of Harvard's Stoughton Hall. The following year he donated land, designed the building, and oversaw construction of a meetinghouse for the new Brattle Street Church. Both the new college and the meetinghouse physically represented the new intellectual and religious trends of anglicanization.

Cotton Mather had long been wary of Thomas Brattle, and he was wary of Brattle's form of anglicanization. Cotton was in favor of British culture. He believed that the Indians should be urged to adopt English language and culture. As a commissioner of the New England Company, Cotton approved of using missionary money to help pay for Brattle's new Stoughton Hall. The question was, anglicanization to what end? He and his father energetically promoted unity among Protestants and worked to bring British Presbyterians, Baptists, and Congregationalists together into a formal union. A union of British Protestants was good. But Increase and Cotton did not want the Congregationalist churches of Massachusetts to be subsumed into mere British Protestantism. Cotton wanted Protestants to unite in affirming their freedom in Christ. He feared that the "innovators" surrounding Thomas Brattle were abandoning their gospel freedom and replacing it with conformity.

Freedom was a deep and powerfully biblical notion for Cotton Mather. Beginning in the late 1690s, Cotton became the leader — he privately wrote that he was the sole leader — of an alternative party of "Eleutherians." This meant freemen, or libertarians, who embrace the fullness of the gospel life. For several decades he referred to this Eleutherian party as "the evangelical interest." Cotton used the terms "Eleutherians" and "evangelical interest" to designate the people that rallied to his call to hot-spirited, Bible-based Christianity, anxious for perfect freedom in Christ. St. Paul in Romans 8, using the Greek term *eleutheria,* declared that Christians have been freed from the law of sin and death. Cotton believed that the Brattle and Leverett circle had been freed, but they had faltered in their pursuit of the fullness of freedom. Instead of being hot-spirited, they were lukewarm. They promoted the Protestant interest of the empire, but not the evangelical interest.

In *Eleutheria,* Cotton's 1698 history of the idea of Christian reformation in Britain, he wrote of the constant tension in Christian history between Eleutherians and Idumaeans. The latter term was derived from the people of Edom in the Old Testament. They were the descendants of Esau, who shortsightedly sold his birthright to Jacob. Cotton compared them to Lot's wife, who, when fleeing from certain death in Sodom, foolishly looked back even though God had told her not to look back. The Idumaeans had settled in land outside the Promised Land and had hindered the progress of Moses and the freedom-seeking Hebrews.

Idumaeans in British history were the Christians who faltered in the pursuit of the fullness of freedom. Jesus had come to set Christians

This 1726 print was drawn by William Burgis at the end of Cotton Mather's life. Note that without the "university" charter that the Mathers desired, Burgis correctly titled this "The Colleges in Cambridge in New England." The building on the left is Harvard College, which was constructed while Cotton was a student. Cotton lived in this building and spent many happy hours in its second-floor library. In the middle is Stoughton College, the building that the Mathers pushed to have built as part of an idealistic program to make the college "greater and better." Designed by Thomas Brattle, it was the first college in America to be built in the Georgian style, the style that became nearly ubiquitous for American colleges. On the right is Massachusetts College, built in 1720. This third is the only one of these buildings still standing. At the time this print was published, Cotton Mather was still pressing for the progress of Harvard. He was especially successful in helping the college retain a Jewish convert to teach Hebrew and fill its first professorial chair in natural science. His highest goal was to make Harvard more like the progressive University of Halle in Saxony. (Used by permission of the Massachusetts Historical Society)

free and encouraged them to create churches wherever two or three were gathered. King Lucius in the second century had encouraged free creation of churches in Britain. But later, Roman Catholicism arrived and British Idumaeans freely relinquished their ecclesiastical liberty and conformed to the will of a Roman pope, who sent bishops to administer Roman rites. Later in the 1500s there was a revolution by British Eleutherians — Protestants who wanted their freedom back. However, Idumaeans among the Protestants did not want full freedom and preferred subjugation to bishops and liturgical forms derived from Rome. On the ladder to freedom, Cotton believed that Presbyterians also faltered. They clung to rote prayers, liturgical forms, and regional power over individual churches. According to him, it was the Congregationalist churches that were the most intent upon gospel freedom. Cotton wrote that between 1620 and 1640, New England was "peopled with *Evangelical churches*" — Eleutherian churches. In the post-Puritan period of religious freedom, Cotton watched for signs of Idumaean-like thinking in New England. Cotton, like his father, supported Protestant unity among various types of churches, but he considered it his special duty to keep encouraging all Protestants, especially Congregationalists, to continue the hot pursuit of evangelical freedom.

Beginning in the late 1690s and throughout the rest of his life, Cotton had a scale in his mind upon which he rated the Protestants who peopled the various churches of New England. All, in his mind, should be expected to be Eleutherians. Some were obvious Idumaeans who obstructed the path to freedom. Many were confused and needed to be pointed in the right direction. A few were "True Eleutherians" who would not be held back and wanted to win the gospel race to what Cotton called the "top of Christianity." Cotton believed his job as minister in New England was to encourage all to be True Eleutherians. In the introduction to the *Ratio Disciplinae Fratrum,* written during the first decade of the 1700s, Cotton heaped scorn on those who chose to limit their freedom. Those Protestants who insisted on conformity between all the churches were "unreasonable sons of Procrustes." (Procrustes insisted people should fit beds, not beds should fit people.) They were "the narrow-souled and imperious bigots for uniformity." It was ironic, Cotton believed, that people and churches were actually conforming to society in the name of freedom.

For Cotton, the creation of the Brattle Street Church was a retreat from evangelical freedom. The church's "undertakers" architecturally conformed to a British style, liturgically conformed to a Catholic practice of prayer, ecclesiastically conformed to an Anglican notion of membership, and, maybe worst of all, sneakily hired a minister who had been ordained Presbyterian-style in England. Cotton did not think any of this undermined the validity of the Brattle Street Church as a Protestant church, but it did not show free thinking. Instead it showed a lack of heart and a willingness to conform to respectable London values. The motive for it all seemed lukewarm rather than hot.

Cotton railed against the founders of the new church in his *Diary,* and in a burst of private anger, he attributed the actions of the Brattle

Street innovators to Satan. Rather melodramatically, he further wrote in the *Diary* that the defense of New England churches now "must unavoidably fall on me."

Cotton was not at his best in this tempest-in-a-teapot about the Brattle Street Church. Happily, overt antagonism quickly disappeared. Cotton and his father were anxious to maintain ecclesiastical unity among those of the Protestant interest even when they discerned important differences between churches. What is important to see here is that Cotton perceived himself as representing a distinct group within the larger Protestant whole. He called this group "Eleutherian" and described it as "the evangelical interest." He was up against the Idumaean tendencies of the Protestant interest, the inability to sustain the pursuit of gospel freedom. Anglicanization was not wrong, but it was dangerously tepid.

After the witch trials Cotton Mather had become a standard-bearer for a my-utmost-for-his-highest type of Christianity, which moderates saw as too extreme. In March of 1698, a gentleman who had recently arrived from England approached Cotton, provocatively saying that all the good people in Boston honored him but "all the base people . . . hate you and can't give you a good word." In June, Cotton wrote obliquely that "all the Malice of Earth and Hell" was arrayed against him. The following summer, after publishing several books in London, he wrote that he was credibly informed that the Bishop of London had requested negative information about Cotton from his curates in Boston. Soon after, someone else told him that some men belonging to the Church of England "were privately hatching a plot to ruin me."

In response, Cotton monitored his reputation, trying to gauge whether it was being undermined. In September of 1698, during his annual circuit preaching and lecturing at churches and towns up through Salem to Ipswich, Cotton noted that there was a "great flocking to hear me." He reminded himself that this was a vanity and that he should not develop a "taste for popular applause." But applause gauged his reputation, and a pastor needs to have a good reputation if he is to be effective. He later rode out to Reading to preach and happily noted that the meetinghouse there was packed with listeners who even came in from other towns to hear him. Two months later he recorded that he preached to over four thousand at an execution sermon. Throughout 1699 he recorded several times that his reputation remained unblemished and appreciatively noted the large numbers supporting his ministry. His reputation remained strong despite stories he was hearing about people purposefully trying to undermine him.

Herein lies the birth of the evangelical tradition in America: A coalition of ministers and laypeople rallied to Cotton Mather's call to a zealous, freedom-loving, Bible-focused Protestantism that was open to spiritual activities and communications. This was not a doctrinal coalition because no essential doctrines of Christianity were being debated. Essentially it was a fellowship of those who appreciated Cotton Mather's biblical priorities and his belief that New England was a battleground in the spiritual war between Satan and the triune God. Cotton believed that he had a particular God-given role in the battle — as a target for the opposition. "I am feeble," he wrote in his *Diary,* "and in this town I have many enemies, indeed all the enemies of the evangelical interest are mine."

Was Cotton Mather crazy? Was he paranoid? Were the enemies of gospel freedom really focused against him? The best question here is to ask whether Cotton Mather was actually at the center of a popular movement in New England that perceived itself distinct from lukewarm Protestantism. More to the point, did Cotton Mather have enough influence to tug so effectively against the imperial Protestantism in New England that we should believe him to be the first significant figure of the American evangelical movement?

It appears so. At age thirty-six he was New England's most popular pastor. Indeed, he would soon be the most famous American in the British Empire. The Bishop of London was already keeping an eye on him, and soon, with the publication of the *Magnalia Christi Americana,* he would become well known among scholars throughout Europe. On preaching tours into the countryside, crowds would press in to hear him. He was New England's most intellectually and spiritually dynamic pastor. His ministry through books was expanding as he published internationally in several languages. Locally he had so many ready readers that publishers would sometimes ask him after a service for the right to print the sermon he had just given. Printers in London knew they could sell his books. The Earl of Bellomont, the new royal governor of Massachusetts, used Cotton as a speech writer. A pastor in Medfield told Cotton that a godly eighty-year-old woman in his congregation had lost her hearing. After reading one of Cotton's accounts of miracles, her faith grew strong in God's healing power and her hearing returned.

Cotton Mather could not be ignored. It mattered what he said and thought. By 1699 Cotton knew this as much as everybody else in Boston. People of an evangelical interest looked to him for leadership.

It is important that we don't assume that Cotton's use of the term "evangelical" is equivalent to later uses of the term. The American evangelical tradition is dynamic, especially after it unfolds itself over three centuries into transatlantic and global forms. As a tradition it has core characteristics and peripheral features that are identifiable through time. Most scholars trace the American stream of the evangelical tradition back to the split between supporters of Great Awakening revivals and non-supporters. The American evangelical tradition entails much more than just revivals, but we see in the revivals certain core aspects of early American evangelical thought — most particularly an openness to the winds of the Holy Spirit, the experience of answered prayer, a biblical focus on Jesus as savior in and through history, and a readiness to judge, negatively or positively, the spiritual temperature of a pastor or church. Cotton Mather encouraged each of these.

An All-Day-Long Faith

Richard Lovelace published in 1979 probably the best and most empathetic study of Cotton Mather's beliefs: *The American Pietism of Cotton Mather: Origins of American Evangelicalism.* Lovelace emphasized how Mather's notion of an "American pietism" linked to the Lutheran pietism blossoming in European universities, especially the model of August Hermann Francke at the University of Halle. Cotton Mather began corresponding with Francke in 1707, and was much encouraged by Francke's success as an all-around Christian who merged being a university professor with founding institutions to help the poor, preaching the gospel with meeting people's physical needs, and balancing inner personal piety with an outward social conscience. It is tempting to see the origins of the evangelical tradition in this fruitful correspondence, but Lovelace was careful not to say that Cotton's notions of piety were learned from Francke. What Cotton saw in Francke and in Halle was a social and institutional system of piety more developed than what he had already begun creating in Boston.

The American evangelical tradition is best seen as beginning in the middle 1690s when most of New England's leadership became caught up with stabilizing the province's politics and religion after the arrival of a new royal charter and the completion of the Salem witch trials. Cotton Mather, who at the time was in his thirties, was growing into the self-aware leader he would increasingly become. There was a period of months in 1699-1700, while he was serving as speech writer to the Earl of Bellomont, when Cotton thought he was in the inner circle of the new royal governor. Cotton had a heady moment when his words were spoken and published by the representative of the king and queen. In that speech, Cotton declared the empire's commitment to "the Protestant interest." But he was not the kind of man who could comfortably serve imperial politics. Later that year, while in his high pulpit leading public prayer, he felt his "heart strangely melted" by "an irradiation from heaven" that God was at work against the enemies of the Reformation throughout the world. By this time, Cotton was realizing the extent to which people were listening to him. He had already begun to fear the complacency he saw developing among the Protestants around him. God, he believed, had not called him to be a moderate and careful speechwriter, nor an encourager of comfortable religion. He was called to stir the hearts of people. If we want to look for the origin of the American evangelical tradition, we should look to Cotton's ministry in the North End and his more wide-spread preaching in the years surrounding 1700.

Beginning in the 1690s, and for many years after, Cotton would make a vacation preaching-tour every fall, traveling north from Salem through Wenham up to Ipswich. He felt a deep affinity with the people in that region, and he enjoyed riding his horse through the beautiful countryside. On these tours people from nearby towns would crowd together in one meetinghouse to hear him. Although this yearly vacation was geographically limited to a small region north of Boston, Mather treated these tours as a great opportunity to communicate widely with all the people of New England. For example, in the fall of 1701 when preparing for his trip to Ipswich, Cotton "propounded unto [himself]" that he should prepare two discourses that would be of "some advantage to the evangelical interests." As was common practice for him, he decided he would both preach them and publish them. The two sermons would be joined together as one small, thin, unbound book. He would pay for the printing himself. It was the equivalent of the kind of thicker pamphlet that one finds displayed on a rack in the foyer of any active church today. Having a good number printed, Cotton passed them out to families on his circuit ride and sent them out to friendly pastors for distribution to families in other towns. In this way his messages were much more widely disseminated than when he just preached to the churches on his tour. As was also normal for him, he likewise gave copies to ship captains engaged in Atlantic and coastal trade, asking that they pass them on to the ministers who resided in whatever ports their ships visited. In that less distracted era, Cotton was confident that the families who received the book would read it aloud after dinner, then pass the book on to another family for them to read aloud the next night. The book was meant to be ephemeral in the best sense of the term — important, read, discussed, and passed on. The pamphlet lost its purpose if given a sedentary place on a bookshelf.

Cotton wrote and printed many such books, but this one he devised at a crucial time for the specific purpose of supporting what he felt was the beleaguered evangelical interest in 1701. The two sermons were joined under the title *The Christian and His Calling.*

The first sermon in the book begins by noting that the fear of God is a pursuit of long-term, *ultimate happiness.* This pursuit involves head, hands, and lips, but is primarily a "heart business." It is a daily walk to the very top of Christianity. It is an all-day-long faith that begins with a morning "closet time" dedicated to Bible-reading and prayer. Progress through the day is marked regularly by holiness of thought, word, and deed. Prayers spring forth at random moments. Cotton wrote that with these random prayers we "shoot the arrows of our desires away to heaven," and "happy is the man that hath his quiver filled with these arrows." All day long the evangelical Christian should be promoting happiness in others, especially among children and servants in the household. At the end of the day the whole household should pray together after reading portions from the Bible. Yes, Cotton noted, each day will have its sufferings. "A Christian is a cross bearer and no day ordinarily comes to a Christian without its cross." But it is God who sends these crosses, and God looks out for our best interest.

Such is the "general calling" to all Christians. But Cotton described it as only one oar in our rowboat. We need two oars so as to properly proceed toward eternal blessedness. The second oar, described in the second of the two sermons, is a "personal calling," or a particular calling to each Christian. "God has placed us as in a common hive," and we each must do our part for the whole. Each of us needs to husband our time. We need to avoid financial debt, keep our promises, and be content with our situations. No job should be thought too small. We must especially value our neighbors — and here Cotton noted that his own neighbors were often sailors who had their own special calling and particular issues concerning the daily living of their faith. Sabbath keeping, for example, was sometimes impossible for sailors. Overall, every person must find his or her particular calling and use commonsense in determining how best to serve God with it. "A Christian," Cotton advised, "should with piety follow his occupation," but should not let piety swallow up his daily occupational obligations. Every Christian, even Sabbath-breaking sailors, must work out his personal calling while remaining in Christ's service as a member of the common hive.

But most people do not have a sailor's excuse for Sabbath breaking. Cotton insisted that the first commitment of people pursuing their particular vocations was to enter God's rest on the Sabbath. Every Christian should honor the Lord's Day by attending worship services. As for the rest of the week: "Let obedience to God be the spring and strain of all your business." Be humble: "When you follow your business have your dependence on God for the succeeding of it." And be blessed: "May you all follow your good occupation, and may goodness and mercy follow you all in your occupation."

At his core, Cotton Mather was not what we would call an elitist. He was a populist. His vision of holiness had a common touch and his appeal to listeners and readers was his emphasis on the practical. He liked to compare human life to the work of bees. He shared in the classical tradition of appreciating life within a hive — a social life mysteriously productive of goodness and honey. For Cotton, the evangelical interest should be broadly appealing to the masses. When he questioned the value of his ministry in his *Diary,* he found reassurance in the crowds who came to listen to him and the publishers that wanted his books. He took particular comfort in the "extraordinary auditories" — the crowds who showed up to listen to him — when he was invited to preach outside of Boston. His greatest comfort was his own congregation in North Square. From the pulpit he consistently saw before him a packed house of fifteen hundred souls seeking to learn more about the gospel and the life of holiness from him. On one occasion in 1701, he delivered a sermon about shunning bad company. Afterward, he called for the members of the church's "Young-Men's Meeting" to come hear more from him that evening. That night Cotton counted near one hundred "serious devout young men" who showed up to hear more about "the danger and folly of bad company." A few months later, after noting that over the years he had created thirteen or fourteen "private meetings" where people in his neighborhood regularly gathered for prayer and Bible study, he contemplated the fact that he knew of no other minister on earth at that time who had charge over so many people. "Lord," he prayed, "assist me to value and improve my precious opportunities!"

Value them he did. Cotton embraced his preaching ministry more than any other of his many activities. When ministers invited him into their pulpits, when crowds of people walked miles to hear him, and when large numbers of young people responded to his call, he knew God was blessing his ministry. Of course Cotton took great pride in his fast-growing list of publications and his international correspondence with famous scholars, but these did not encourage and justify his ministry in the way crowds did. In his mind, the gospel was an appealing prospect offering happy life and healthy freedom within mutually uplifting fellowship. If proclaimed properly, people should want to hear this good news. It was his great blessing to have the opportunity to reach so many.

Charles Morton, the *Spirit of Man,* and Sanctification

The call to a happy life is a call to a higher life. Mere Protestantism is a good foundation, but Cotton wrote that the evangelical interest called a person to the top of Christianity. The Bible vaguely calls this rise to the top "sanctification," the progression beyond mere belief when people actively seek holiness. The precise definition, process, and levels of sanctification have long been debated within Christianity. As far back as when Paul questioned "Why do I do what I do?" and Augustine wondered why he kept moving deeper into Christianity, the call to sanctification has encouraged theories of human psychology. Probably the most famous psychological study of this sort in early American evangelical tradition was published a couple of decades after the death of Cotton Mather: Jonathan Edwards' *A Treatise Concerning Religious Affections.* But if Cotton Mather was the first American evangelical leader, then the first American evangelical study of psychology was Charles Morton's *Spirit of Man* published in Boston in 1692. It was the first book on psychology published in America. Cotton Mather wrote the introduction to the book and emphasized Morton's point that the promotion of holiness and happiness is the "whole work of sanctification" upon a spirit in man. Cotton was not writing poetically about this "spirit in man." Charles Morton and Cotton Mather believed that there is something in humans, something that is a middle substance between body and soul, that Cotton called the *Nishmath-Chajim,* or "Breath of Life." Cotton and Charles Morton had been talking together about this division within human psychology long into the nights before publication of Morton's book. They agreed that this middle substance affected a person's temperament and had a temperature. Their study of this middle substance offered a psychological foundation for a range of personal traits, but was especially important for understanding the psychology of those who pursued sanctification.

Charles Morton was revered by all the intellectual elite in New England. Increase Mather had begged him to come to New England after Morton's highly influential academy in Newington Green, London, was forced to shut its doors. After his arrival in 1686 the tutors at Harvard started assigning Morton's innovative and influential textbooks on physics, logic, ethics, and pneumatology. Morton's textbooks on ethics and pneumatology analyzed the interrelationships between psychological "faculties" (intellect, will, and sensitive appetites) and included an appendix on the body-soul questions raised by the renowned French philosopher and mathematician René Descartes. Morton's texts were transcribed and studied by Elisha Williams, who taught them to the young Jonathan Edwards. Though it is unclear whether Edwards ever read Morton's *Spirit of Man,* he was almost certainly exposed to some of Morton's views on psychology. What is certain, however, is that Cotton Mather deeply appreciated the book as a way of explaining his own hot temperament, and the hotter temperaments that distinguished those who lived out an all-day-long faith.

Morton got his idea of three parts constituting human wholeness primarily from Paul's first letter to the Thessalonians: "And the very God of Peace sanctify you wholly, and I pray God your whole SPIRIT, and SOUL, and BODY be preserved blameless unto the coming of our Lord Jesus Christ" (5:23). Morton then noted, as Wesleyans would later emphasize, that the term "wholly" in Paul's Greek is best translated as "wholly perfectly." Morton noted learned debates about the meaning of "spirit," but by using various biblical passages he showed that a person's spirit is distinguished from his or her body and soul. Bodies are complex physical entities — touchable, such as when Thomas touched the risen Jesus. Souls hold a person's faculties of will and understanding. The spirit is a kind of third entity that is the seat of human temperament, inclination, and genius. Sanctification is facilitated mainly by the spirit, rather than the soul or body.

Morton believed the spirit is in all people, whether Christian or not. It is a middle substance of some sort that can be categorized by its various types that appear in various people. Some Christians, he noted, are cold and cranky, others hot and volatile, and many have a moderate spirit. Morton's *Spirit of Man* can be read as a guide to psychological self-reflection, and Cotton saw it as an aid for those of the evangelical interest pursuing holiness. Each individual needs to understand his or her inner spirit in order to better apply themselves to holiness. This is why sanctification begins in one's spirit no matter what type of spirit a person has.

Christians need to aspire to perfection and methodically pursue it, but perfection is not a cookie-cutter model. Different spirits have different marks of sanctification. God created each person with a unique spirit but each person's actions can influence his or her spirit. One very important example that Morton almost offhandedly notes is that some people have very even and balanced spirits. This can be good or bad. There is a "seeming virtue" in calmness of will and moderation of affections, but such evenness of mind can also slide into a lack of concern about one's own soul or the souls of others. "This," says Morton, "is the odious *lukewarmness* which God will spew out of his mouth." Moderate Christians need to be wary of their moderateness.

A person can also affect his or her own inclinations and temperament with education, discipline, and prayer. It is hard for a cranky person to become cheerful, but it is possible with God's help. The idea that one's spirit can be affected by education, discipline, and prayer also means that an unregulated spirit can change for the worse. Each disposition of spirit has its own dangers. Inquisitiveness tends to push one toward skepticism if not bolstered by education, discipline, and prayer. Worldly wisdom, if not directed toward God, can easily be turned by Satan into "mischievous counsels." A tendency to be mournful can be put to higher purpose if one disciplines it to support regular prayer. A hot and volatile spirit, although it might be directed to glorify God, can fall easily into "huffs and hectors" and pulled into sin by Satan.

Morton died in 1698, but Cotton carried Morton's psychologically sophisticated view into his life as a scholar-pastor. Cotton saw many in

New England pursuing a moderation that could easily fall into a genteel lukewarmness. Moderate men, increasingly around the year 1700, were patting each other on the back for being "catholick." The Brattle Street Church waved the flag of moderation in downtown Boston. Cotton perceived himself to have a "personal calling" from God, a calling to encourage people, no matter what their exact category of spirit, to avoid lukewarmness and aspire to sanctification. He was not like his father, who preferred to rail in general against the decline of Puritan piety; rather, Cotton dedicated himself to encouraging individuals to first "know thyself," then programmatically, methodically, with an all-day-long faith, steer themselves toward the top of Christianity.

"God Threw My Daughter in the Fire"

In the *Diary* entry for January 2, 1699, Cotton wrote: "Alas for my sin, the just God threw my daughter into the fire!" Taking into account that Cotton Mather's *Diary* was not written day-by-day but, instead, was a yearly compilation, this statement was not merely an emotional outburst. It was well considered and reflects how he thought about God.

It is easy to imagine the scene: a cold Monday and his three young daughters with him in his study. Cotton called the girls Katy, Nibby, and Nanny, his "little birds." Cotton sits at his cluttered desk with several open books stacked near his elbow. Katy, twelve years old and precocious, is sitting on a chair near the fire reading to her sisters, four and two years old, lying in front of her on the floor. Cotton, not easily distracted, is not bothered by Katy's reading and is lost in his work. Abigail, his pregnant wife, is downstairs in the kitchen. Needing something, Cotton stands up and says he will be right back as he walks out the door. While he is away, Hannah, fidgeting on the floor, starts to stand up but loses her balance and topples into the fire. Chaos ensues. The girls all scream as Katy grabs Hannah out of the fire. Cotton comes running in. By the time Abigail gets into the room, Cotton is on the floor with Hannah screaming in his arms. Katy and Nibby are standing at each of his shoulders looking down in shock. A servant is sent running to Cotton's parents' house for help. Cotton and Abigail try to calm little Hannah, but each is horrified by what they see. The right side of her face is severely burned along with her right hand and arm. She could die from these wounds.

Cotton and Abigail were distraught throughout the next week as the two-year-old suffered in constant and terrible pain. Cotton wrote that he "kept pouring out my prayers to God, for his mercies unto the child, and the rest of the family." On Friday he spent the day in his study praying. Hannah's situation was a "Rebuke of Heaven" and after focusing his mind on the sufferings of Christ and the mercy of God, he set himself "to cry unto Heaven for the welfare of my children, and my whole family, on all accounts." On that day he "obtained mercy for all my children." God gave him assurance that his prayers were heard. For his "scorched child" he received there in the study a particular confidence from God: "She shall not only be speedily and happily cured, but she shall be blessed throughout eternal ages. God will make her one of his own children. God will distinguish her with marks of his everlasting love. The fire that has wounded the child, has added a strong fire and force to the zeal of my prayer for her. And God has now raised my prayer for her to this degree of particular faith in her behalf."

Writing about this in his *Diary,* Cotton spoke directly to a future Hannah through his book. He expected his children to read his *Diary* someday. He wanted her to read his thoughts about her wounds and realize God's eternal blessing. She, like him, should give thanks that God had cast her into the fire. The incident had enflamed his prayers for her, and God had revealed his plans for her. The Sunday following the accident Cotton preached about Hannah's fall. His daughter was still in pain and would be maimed and disfigured for life, but he told his congregation that he was confident that God's providence was in the smallest actions and accidents. God's providence extended even to sparrows — even to his little birds.

Cotton Mather never thought to himself, "God wouldn't do that"; he never responded to human suffering by asking why God had not stepped in to rectify the situation; Cotton never tried to protect God from responsibility for everything; and he never assured the mother of a suffering baby that a loving God would not do this to a baby. God was not trapped by a logic that said that contraries — human freedom and divine sovereignty — could not exist at the same time in the same situation. Certainly God was not trapped by dictionary definitions of goodness and love. The picture of God in the Bible was big: "My thoughts are not your thoughts, neither are your ways my ways"; "The Lord is in his holy temple; let all the earth be silent before him." Cotton had no problem thinking himself small and believing there were more mysteries in life than understandings. He appreciated Paul's picture of God as potter and people as clay.

Katy and Hannah clung to each other for the rest of their lives. Neither ever married. After their mother died, the two of them in turn clung to Cotton, and the three were nearly inseparable. Hannah's deeply scarred face and hand was a daily reminder to Katy and Cotton of the result of a moment's inattention. But her marks also reminded them that "God will distinguish her with marks of his everlasting love."

Cotton was no stranger to suffering and disappointment. Of his fifteen children he buried thirteen. One of his boys was born without an anus, and all Cotton and Abigail could do was sit next to him, praying, while they watched him die. Cotton did not question why God would cause a situation like that to occur. He never tried to logically work out how a good God can allow babies to suffer. Cotton was humble. God was God. God was good. Cotton's job was to trust and obey. At times, as with his Hannah, he would be overwhelmed by a "particular faith" that assured him of something. During the decade after Hannah's fall he experienced particular faiths that his father would be called back to England and that his young son would eventually become a pastor. Both of these particular faiths proved false. Such disappointments, however, did not undermine his belief.

As a pastor, he was more often encouraging than critical or somber. When people came to him afraid for their souls, Cotton tended to be upbeat. In 1702, a young minister, much distressed for his soul, came to Cotton seeking advice. Cotton, sitting at his desk, pointed to a clock on the shelf in his study and asked him what use the young man would put the clock to? Would you use it as a stool to sit on or as firewood for the fire? No, the young man replied. "Well then," Cotton said, "have not you upon your soul a divine workmanship far more excellent than the most curious clock-work in the world?" Did the young minister not want to "serve the interests of the Lord Jesus Christ and slay all sin"? Of course he did. "Such a piece of workmanship," Cotton continued, "as what is wrought in you was never intended to be thrown into the fire of Hell. No, there is no use of it there. God intends you for a heavenly use, undoubtedly."

The Westminster Confession declared that the chief end of man was to glorify God and enjoy him forever. Cotton emphasized the glorifying and enjoying. He found divine sovereignty comforting. The doctrine encouraged joy in all situations. When preaching, Cotton had no interest in confusing the congregation by pitting God's sovereignty in opposition to human freedom. In one of the few instances in his work in which he directly engaged the relationship between divine foreknowledge and human liberty, Cotton declared that the two work "sweetly" together. He further told his readers that he had no interest in logical speculation on the issue: "I have plain people to deal with. And for them, I will make as learned an answer to it as any that I have met with. My answer is 'I cannot tell,' I say, 'I cannot tell.' The best flight of our learning, in such a point as this, is a confession of our ignorance."

Human ignorance and divine mysteries were not to be feared. Cotton found comfort in both. Abigail, Cotton's wife, died soon after the young pastor's visit in 1702. She miscarried on the twenty-fifth of June, and many days and nights of the following month were spent praying at her side. She had given birth to a new baby in late 1699 called Cresy (Increase). Katy was now fifteen, Nibby seven, and the fire-scarred Nanny five. Several times during her illness Cotton felt what he called "the blessed breezes of a particular faith" assuring him that his wife would live. But repeatedly he "submitted unto the sorrowful consequences of a rejected prayer, and a defeated faith, and a desolate broken family." Abigail hung on into August. One night he stayed up with her so that he could watch her die, but she continued to linger in pain. Family and neighbors rotated at her bedside day and night. After a turn for the better, she eventually died at age thirty-two on the first day of December. Cotton and the congregation of North Church loved her very much and mourned deeply. As a great honor to Abigail, North Church purchased for her the prominent tomb that still stands at Copp's Hill. Today people visit the tomb as the resting place of Cotton and his father, but they should remember that the tomb was first created by a congregation that loved their pastor's wife.

Writing later in his *Diary* to his children about her death, he noted the sting of "a miscarriage of a particular faith." God, he thought, had given him assurances that she would live. "It may be," he wrote, "that the Lord will ere long enable me to penetrate further into the nature, meaning, and mystery of a particular faith; however, I have met with enough to awaken in me a more exquisite caution." Through all his sufferings and misunderstandings Cotton clung to God. If Cotton misinterpreted God's communication sometimes, it was because of his own weakness.

Three months after Abigail's death an "airy" twenty-year-old gentlewoman proposed marriage to the forty-year-old Cotton. She said she appreciated his accomplishments. Cotton knew in his head that widowers frequently play the fool, but this young woman's appeal was not a matter of the head. She was young and comely, and she knew how to manipulate him. She even convinced him that he had a responsibility to marry her, that in marriage to him she would be spiritually uplifted. Cotton almost fell for it. Friends of Cotton interceded and steered him away from her. A few months later, Cotton married a thirty-year-old widow who lived a couple of houses down from his own house on Hanover Street. The former Elizabeth Hubbard brought with her into the Mather household a young son about the same age as Cresy. Cotton and his four children welcomed Elizabeth and her son into the family and the seven of them settled in together as a newly blended family.

Thwarted from the Presidency of Harvard

As much as Cotton energetically embraced his job as pastor of a large, diverse, and successful urban church, he, like many pastors who have come after him, was seduced by the thought of being a college president. Here it was not his friends who interceded and steered him away; rather, it was his enemies who saved him from this seduction.

At that time Harvard was a small backwater school with no firm legal foundation, no professors, and about fifty students. What appealed to Cotton was the *idea* of Harvard. Cotton believed his own glowing history of the little college. He believed he could fulfill his father's failed aspiration to make it into a great "American university." He believed that as president he could manage, intellectually and spiritually, New England's transition from Puritanism into the Enlightenment.

It was a foolish dream. The Harvard presidency, as his father knew, was little more than a hole in which to get trapped. Political realities within the British Empire had to be negotiated. A coalition of the political elite agreed that what Harvard needed was stability, not vision. Harvard, it must be remembered, was an offense to the imperial educational establishment. The president's job was not to guide an intellectual and spiritual transition; rather, the job was to hold the middle ground and not ruffle any feathers. Cotton was incapable of aspiring to mundane stability. Cotton should have learned from his father's experience that a college is different from a church. A church will follow a spirit-filled leader who will risk all in pursuit of congregational holiness. A college, on the other hand, is more narrow, more encumbered, and necessarily more bland. Education is an industry of the state, even when it is fired from within by aspirations of the liberal arts. Harvard needed John Leverett, Cotton's rather stuffy but happily authoritarian schoolmate to be president. Wanting the presidency of Harvard was an errata in Cotton's life. But even if it was a foolish aspiration, Cotton learned in the process how popular he was among the people of Massachusetts. Cotton had already begun to believe that large numbers of people beyond his own congregation looked to him as a leader of the evangelical interest. His bid for the Harvard presidency confirmed his self-perception that the evangelical interest looked to him as their most public and worthy leader.

Increase Mather had kept Harvard alive through the dismal years of the early 1670s on through the 80s. Several times he had turned down the presidency, only to be forced to step in and run things at the college. Finally, in 1686 Increase accepted the presidency, but he insisted that he would only be part-time. He was able to retain his position as pastor to Boston's largest church because the college was small and Cotton had begun assisting him.

Harvard's overseers saw a part-time presidency as a reasonable compromise. Soon afterwards, however, the colony needed Increase Mather as an ambassador to England. So between 1688 and 1692 the president of the college was out of the country, and the small student body was left in the hands of the two young tutors, William Brattle and John Leverett. Providing the tutors with advice and counsel was the vice president, Charles Morton, who was not far away in Charlestown.

After Increase returned to America, he resumed his work at both the church and the college. He soon initiated an ambitious new master plan and got his fingers into every aspect of the college's mission, laws, and legal foundation. He first wrote a new charter for the college that was passed by a Massachusetts legislature in 1692. At that time the governor and the legislature were still much under his leadership. In the new charter, Increase consolidated power over the college in a group called the Harvard Corporation, made up of the president, treasurer, and eight fellows. Within a year, Thomas Brattle became treasurer. Cotton Mather, William Brattle, John Leverett, and five other prominent ministers made up the eight fellows. In the new charter, Increase had even created the new motto for what he hoped would soon be a full-fledged university: "For Christ and Church." Increase thought big. He envisioned a Dutch-style university which would take students in at an even younger age and carry them all the way through to advanced degrees. By offering doctorate degrees, Harvard could start producing its own professors and no longer have to rely only on tutors. Increase further hoped to revive Harvard's role at the center of the New England Company's plans for Indian education. Basically Increase believed in centralizing the colony's educational efforts into one institution, and through it, bolstering the distinctive Puritan hope of a unified and in-dependent New England. In the 1690s, Increase worked hard to bring his vision to fruition.

Cotton was fully supportive of his father's vision and often served as his father's secretary, personal assistant, and partner on the Har-vard Corporation. Increase also had the full support of his good friend William Stoughton, who paid for a stately new building, and his vice president, Charles Morton. Together they helped Increase draft an up-graded charter that declared Harvard a university. As a necessary act to jump-start the system, Increase had himself awarded a doctor of divinity degree. Increase saw his doctorate as a preemptive strike on full recognition by the king — "accreditation" in our modern language. Increase had met the king while in England and was confident, proba-bly overconfident, that the king and his men would not take offense at Harvard's presumptuousness. Ultimately, the king never got a chance to be presumed upon. The leading elite of the province thought that Mather was raising a flag that should not be waved. Calling Harvard a university, calling himself a "doctor," and writing a charter that would not allow the king or his bishops to oversee the curriculum could only draw unwanted imperial attention to the province.

Happily, in 1700 the new royal governor, Lord Bellomont, was sur-prisingly friendly to the idea of asking the king to create a rogue univer-sity in New England. The governor even initiated correspondence on the matter with the Lords of Trade. Increase, at this time, soon expected a commission to go to England where he was sure that, if he could speak directly with the king, Harvard would receive its full-fledged, but fully in-dependent, university charter. Cotton daily prayed for his father's wish to come true. Cotton believed that a meeting between his father and the king would solve many of the problems in Massachusetts. Unhappily, the upper house of the Massachusetts legislature, and many other elite friends of the Mathers, disagreed. Samuel Sewall and the Reverend Sam-uel Willard of South Church could appreciate the Mathers' ideals, but they thought that pushing for a new charter at that time put the whole college

Signatures of the Harvard Corporation in 1699. President Increase
Mather is at the top and Cotton Mather second to last. Thomas
Brattle, the treasurer, was not present. Charles Morton had died
the year before. The fellows present were all prominent minis-
ters: James Allen of Boston First Church, Samuel Torrey from
Weymouth, Samuel Willard from Boston South Church, Peter
Thacher from Milton, John Danforth from Dorchester, and Ben-
jamin Wadsworth from Boston First Church. (From Justin Winsor, ed.,
The Memorial History of Boston [Boston: James R. Osgood Company, 1880-81])

at risk. Compromise, even inaction, was the best course. Lie low. Be inof-
fensive. Don't become interesting to the imperial bureaucracy in London.

Many leaders in Massachusetts were happy that the king never
learned that Increase Mather wanted to talk to him. Lord Bellomont's
letter supporting the creation of a Harvard University was conveniently
lost in London's bureaucracy. Increase was subsequently eased out of
Harvard's presidency with the insistence that he be promoted to full-
time president, an office that entailed living full-time in Cambridge.

Increase squirmed and tried to live for a while in Cambridge, but, in the end, he moved back to Boston and relinquished the presidency. Samuel Willard of South Church then took up an interim and part-time presidency that would allow everything to calm down. Supposedly, Harvard's overseers — both the Corporation and the colonial government — were searching for a new president, but nothing was being done to secure one. The goal was achieved — Harvard was quietly staying unobtrusive.

This changed in March of 1703 when the Massachusetts assembly, the lower house of the legislature composed of democratically elected representatives from every town, stuck their nose into Harvard's business by unanimously recommending Cotton Mather be named president. In political language, "the people" had rallied to their candidate. Nothing shows the ongoing popular respect for Cotton Mather in Massachusetts better than this vote.

Six months earlier, Cotton's massive *Magnalia Christi Americana* had arrived in New England after being published in London. Not only was it obvious to any who saw the bulky work that this was an impressive piece of historical scholarship, but readers also found in it Cotton's high aspirations for the future of their churches, their province, and their college. In the *Magnalia* Cotton encouraged readers to strive for post-Puritan Protestant unity while retaining Congregational distinctiveness. The book gathered many accounts of "remarkable providences" that showed God's sovereign concern for the well-being of New England. Cotton offered histories of the Salem witch trials and other demon-possessions that showed that Satan's interests in New England were being held in check by God and good angels. The *Magnalia* heaped praise on the faithful and showed that Christ was at work in the churches, the Indian missions, and the college. It is easy to imagine ministers and magistrates throughout New England gathering around fireplaces, either reading the *Magnalia* out loud to each other or discussing what they had heard about it. Later that summer, after preaching to crowds in Salem and Reading, Cotton noted that a person of quality — but not piety — told him that he was "the most beloved man in all the country." In November he received a letter from across the Atlantic saying that his *Magnalia* was being read "from one end of England to the other." The letter speculated that the book would have great influence upon the "evangelical interests" in Britain. Of course the author of the *Magnalia Christi Americana,* New England's most accomplished Christian scholar, should be the president of a new Harvard University.

But the move to make Cotton president was thwarted by the provincial council and the new governor, Joseph Dudley, a cousin of the Brattles. The council and governor were looking out for the Protestant interest. Dudley would spend his career as governor protecting the colony from the French and tightening relations within the empire. Harvard needed to stay unthreatening to the king's prerogatives. Massachusetts needed to be on its best behavior in the eyes of the London bureaucracy. The headship of the college could not be handed over to Cotton Mather precisely because he was an internationally famous scholar and populist candidate.

The resolution for Cotton to assume the presidency was ignored as long as the elderly Reverend Willard remained in the interim part-time post. When Willard died four years later, the governor and council were able to negotiate with the assembly so as to give support to John Leverett for president. He was a safe candidate. He was a lawyer with no reputation for being zealous about anything.

If Cotton had actually become president of Harvard, he would have probably tried to change the college by imitating the University of Halle in Saxony where Herman Francke was creating a new model university. Francke was an inspiring scholar-administrator. Cotton wanted to be an American Francke and wanted the Harvard curriculum to follow Halle's by teaching the full range of classical liberal arts while also promoting pietistic faith, social compassion, and humanitarian action. Cotton wrote a student handbook, *Manuductio ad Ministerium,* that described his educational goals. Like Francke, Cotton believed that a liberal arts education should teach the highest ideals of intellect and wisdom along with social responsibility and humanitarian action.

Cotton's handbook insisted that students should be well read. Cotton was a voracious reader and wanted to lead scholars by being a scholar. His library was huge, and he recommended that students should create and prize their own libraries. Cotton often gave away books to students. He would, at times, box up a collection of books and then give the box to a young minister whose church was out on the frontier. Cotton loved to own books, but much of his reading was done standing up in bookstalls reading books he did not buy. He would dig through crates of new books arriving from Europe. Much to the chagrin of the bookstall owners on bustling Dock Square, Cotton would read for an hour from an expensive book, then pull out a private notebook into which he transcribed long passages. People milling about would have smiled to see Cotton midst the noise and smells of the wharf and market once again, contortedly balancing a large volume in the crook of his arm while also trying to write in his notebook. There was the town's famous pastor-scholar, visible to everyone, living the scholarly life to which students were supposed to aspire. He would have led the students at Harvard by doing.

The books Cotton appreciated most were books he called "hives" and he believed them to be essential for improving the education at Harvard. These "hives" were expansive anthologies that hummed with the latest writings by the latest scholars. Several of the largest books that Cotton "wrote," such as the *Magnalia Christi Americana,* the *Christian Philosopher,* and the *Biblia Americana,* are actually hives — American hives meant to engage in the great intellectual conversations of Europe. Cotton believed readers hit the jackpot when they read these types of books that were filled with long quotes from multiple authors. Such volumes drew students into scholarly conversations going on in Europe. He believed that Harvard should be buzzing with the newest ideas and discoveries. He did not think that students should necessarily *believe* all the newest ideas and discoveries. However, he did believe that students and faculty at Harvard should be discussing them.

As much as Cotton Mather wanted Harvard students to be discussing the newest ideas about natural science, philosophy, and theology in the Harvard dining room, he was especially intent in his handbook to recommend study of his favorite discipline: history. Cotton advocated the study of history as "one of the most needful and useful accomplishments for a man that would serve God." He recommended reading "the best we have" of histories, such as Pierre Bayle's *Historical and Critical Dictionary,* one of the great anthologies of the era. Cotton highly recommended it as "a work to be wondered at!" Like many advocates of history in his era, Cotton thought it important for student-historians to learn how "to believe with discretion." Histories need to be read with a critical eye, especially an eye on the lookout for national or religious bias.

Under Cotton, Harvard might have become a uniquely innovative university known for being Bible-oriented, critically engaged, intellectually groundbreaking, and ethnically diverse. It is likely that in his presidency Cotton would have revived the vision of Harvard having an Indian College and expanded Harvard's welcome to the most accomplished graduates from his North End grammar school for Blacks. With his own money and time, Cotton long promoted grammar school education for all Indians and Blacks. The best and the brightest of these students he hoped would become teachers and pastors — primarily returning back to their own communities. Cotton believed in the fundamental equality of all humans and had no desire to limit access to education or to inhibit anyone from fully realizing his or her intellectual capacities. Given Cotton's energy, breadth of vision, and openness to the Republic of Letters, Harvard could have become an amazingly dynamic university under his presidency.

As it turned out, Harvard became unremarkable. During the Leverett years the numbers grew, but the college settled into a comfortable gentility. Henry Flynt, who became the central figure of the faculty during the Leverett years, exemplifies the slumber of Harvard. He was a man of indeterminate Christianity and low aspirations, yet Leverett appreciated his stability even when the overseers of Harvard raised eyebrows at his dubious piety. When Cotton Mather was promoting the reading of Bayle and the best histories and was himself transcribing Jacques Basnage's highly sophisticated study of the history of Jews on three continents, Flynt produced a boring and perfunctory catechism of world history and geography for students at Harvard. No wonder the best Harvard students continued to visit Cotton's study when in Boston. Thomas Prince, the most interesting and innovative scholar of the next generation, a man who graduated from Leverett's and Flynt's Harvard, looked to Cotton Mather as his mentor.

An important matter to note: Cotton in his *Diary* wrote of his "enemies" during this time, but we should not raise this above what it was. We should remember that Boston in 1700 was a small town of maybe seven thousand people. Cambridge was nearby and much smaller. Cotton had regular relations with the Brattles, Leverett, and Dudley as they shared leadership in the public life of New England. Cotton officiated as minister at Leverett's marriage. Many times over the years, Cotton sat in meetings and on podiums with Leverett. In the end, Cotton was one of the pallbearers who carried Leverett to his grave. John Leverett, Thomas Brattle, and Cotton Mather shared in the ongoing leadership of the college, and each was keen for the success of the empire's Protestant interest. What distinguished Cotton Mather from the group was that he tugged, as the populist leader of an evangelical interest, against the gentility of their Protestantism, against the safety of staying in the middle of the empire's current, against lukewarmness.

CHAPTER SIX

A Biblical Enlightenment

1707-1713

Defining "Enlightenment"

Samuel Eliot Morison, in a magisterial history of Harvard published in 1936, breathed a sigh of relief when he finished recounting the story of how Cotton Mather was thwarted from the presidency and John Leverett was securely in place. "The Century of Enlightenment," he wrote, "opened somewhat belatedly in Harvard College on Wednesday the fourteenth of January 1708," the day Leverett was installed as president.

Scholars no longer write so starkly about the enlightenment. We talk of many different types of enlightenments that shade into each other. Several types of enlightenment are rooted in Christian traditions, such as French Roman Catholic Jansenism, Scottish Presbyterian Commonsense, and Saxon Lutheran Pietism. The kind of enlightenment that Leverett supported at Harvard is best described as a provincial British version of a moderate Protestant enlightenment. But just as Cotton Mather led a more zealous evangelical path that tugged against moderate Protestantism, he also led a boisterous "biblical enlightenment" that tugged against the moderate enlightenment.

The various branches of enlightenment share a similarity that gives them their common label: their participants believed they were turning on the lights. The term "enlightenment" was coined to describe a brightening in society and intellectual life that put the "dark ages" behind. The extremists of this transatlantic movement declared that religious superstition was the darkness being left behind and the light of reason was leading rational people away from Bible-based thinking. They insisted that biblical "authority" had kept the world in darkness, and that "free thought" was then beginning to bring better understanding of science and politics. Most people — especially Americans in the first half of the eighteenth century — were not extremists. John Corrigan has shown that many of the young enlightened clergy who graduated from Harvard in the 1690s-1720s sought balance between reason and scriptural authority. They believed in a "supernatural rationalism" that gave space to personal affections for a real Jesus Christ. On the other hand, their pursuit of balance and moderation seemed to Cotton, among many others, to be rooted more in British gentility than heavenly thinking. Scriptures were declared authoritative by everyone, but the moderates preferred to think of God as rather aloof, and they believed that divine truth smoothed the rough edges of the Bible. More than a few of the ministers of the younger generation preached in ways that discouraged spiritual enthusiasm, teaching parishioners not to expect angelic visitations, miraculous healings, or divine interference in the laws of nature. One young pastor encouraged his congregation to have an open mind resting in "aequilibrio."

As a pastor-scholar Cotton Mather embraced many aspects of the enlightenment, but based on his understanding of the Bible he could have never advocated resting in the equilibrium his contemporaries promoted. He encouraged his parishioners and readers to continue to live in the light of the lively and unpredictable God of the Bible. Cotton Mather was easily at the forefront of this more lively type of enlightenment, a type of evangelical enlightenment that would be deepened in the next generation by Jonathan Edwards. Cotton Mather's enlightenment began with his citizenship in the Republic of Letters, his populist love of communication, his appreciation of historical methods of thinking, and his belief that the Bible was the key to the fullest understanding of science and politics available to humans. Cotton did not pit himself as an elite intellectual against the ignorant masses. He called for reasonable people to share with him in the exploration of things both written and observed. Cotton Mather nurtured the forward-looking character of the enlightenment by insisting that the Bible was the most forward looking of all books. The trajectory of history as it moved into the future manifested God's progressive revelation, the fullness of which would be Christ's return and the creation of a New Jerusalem. Cotton was, in many ways, as much a futurist as he was a historian. Uniting the two perspectives was a presentism that encouraged him to be intensely focused on the world around him.

Most scholars will agree that the enlightenment in America is most evident in three core issues of the early eighteenth century. Cotton was a leader in each of these issues. The first was critical engagement with biblical authority. Many scholars in Europe were undermining biblical authority, and Cotton engaged them. The second core issue of the era was the pursuit of knowledge about nature. Science was expanding its influence, and its methods were becoming more complex. Cotton loved keeping up with the new science and even gained a transatlantic reputation in natural philosophy and medicine. Finally, the third core issue of the enlightenment was the promotion of humanitarian acts and institutions that promote widespread freedom and liberty. Here again, Cotton's biblical enlightenment offered what were widely considered in the churches of that era to be the best foundations for progress on this issue.

Eat This Book

Cotton Mather shared the optimism of his age. He believed that knowledge and wisdom would increase in his lifetime as God stirred up "persons of philosophical genius, well furnished with critical learning." But Cotton's optimism tugged against the optimism of the moderate enlightenment because he believed increasing knowledge would come more from listening than any other intellectual skill. God was communicating. People were communicating with each other about their experiences. Critical listening skills would increasingly yield more and better knowledge. Jesus even recommended it in Luke 8: "Consider carefully how you listen." Of course close and careful observation was important, and the progress of natural science depended upon close observation of nature. However, observational skills should not displace listening skills. For example, observation of comets was important. Cotton was fascinated by Edmund Halley's speculation that he could predict the return of what we today call Halley's Comet. But the observation of this amazing fact needed to be augmented by careful listening. God might, Cotton said, be teaching us something with that comet.

The moderate Protestantism of the enlightenment tended to emphasize observation over listening. Leading Protestant thinkers in Europe and the British Empire increasingly assumed that God preferred to be taciturn and aloof. Instead of using words, God would rather just let creation act as a footprint, an indicator of divine orderliness and benevolent watch over creation. From this perspective, God can speak to individuals, send angels as messengers, and even become incarnate in a miracle-working Jesus; however, God did that in the ancient past when civilization was more childlike and needed childlike communications. The Bible is caught in that childlike age and should be understood for what it is. Listening to the Bible for clear and direct information from heaven is a bit childish. God's people, in the more mature and enlightened eighteenth century, should be content with this silent, less intrusive approach.

Cotton Mather could not be content with this. According to him, the Bible's depiction of God indicates a preference to be conversational, gregarious, and daily involved with everything from sustaining natural laws to answering personal prayers. What Cotton considered "the top of practical Christianity" was an all-day-long, back-and-forth, life of conversation with God that begins and ends each day with listening to God specifically speak through the Bible. Comparing what he learned in the Bible with accounts from classical pagans and American Indians, Cotton found confirmation that the cosmos has always been wild with communication and will continue to be wild with communication. Writing in the *Biblia Americana,* Cotton advised against the Quakers' dependence upon an "inner light," not because direct spiritual communications to the soul were untrue, but because they were dangerously true. Cotton himself experienced ecstatic "afflatus" from the Holy Spirit. When some in Boston criticized Cotton for his "enthusiasm," he simply responded "so be it." His warning stemmed from an understanding that all sorts of invisible spirits and communications were vying for human attention. God can speak directly into a person's heart, but so can Satan. Satan is a deceiver, and humans are easily deceived. We should not refuse to listen, but we should also critically examine what we think we heard.

This critical examination uses all the best methods of human reason, but also has to include the higher reasonableness of working with the mysteries of divine communication. Happily, God gives the Bible not only as a divine communication to be examined but also as the guide to critical examination of divine communication. The Bible teaches about the varieties of divine communication, along with teaching how the Bible itself, is to be understood.

Cotton believed that one of the most revealing of the visionary events in the book of Revelation is when an angel — Cotton thought the angel was probably Jesus Christ himself — appeared coming out of heaven clothed in a cloud with a rainbow upon his head and his face like the sun. In the hand of the angel was an unrolled scroll — in Greek an open *biblion* or book. With the messenger raising one hand up to heaven and with the other holding out the book, the voice of God, coming out of heaven, commanded: "Eat this book!"

For those of the evangelical interest who rallied to Cotton Mather's perception of an all-day-long faith, the Bible was not a normal book written long ago, nor was it a childish book from a childish age. The Bible was divine revelation and had to be more than read; it had to be eaten. For Cotton this meant intense and complex listening, a humble type of critical thinking applied to Holy Scripture. Cotton further believed that the deepest understanding of the Bible comes not from simply reading it alone, but from engaging in conversation with other eaters of the Bible. To this end, Cotton began compiling in the early 1690s his most monumental book: the *Biblia Americana*.

The *Biblia Americana* is not one simple book. It is a massive collection of layered dinner table conversations presided over by Cotton, and it is directed toward a mildly skeptical but open-minded inquirer. The book is mostly long quotations from ancient, medieval, and renaissance scholars juxtaposed and unified by Cotton's constant encouragement to listen carefully to the Bible. Cotton presented himself as dinner host when he advertised the book. He told potential buyers that he had "set upon the table . . . a feast of fat things full of marrow, of wines in the lees well refined." Eat not only the Bible, feast also on a compendium of scholarship on the Bible! Just as the Bible itself was a hive out of which the Holy Spirit wonderfully offered honey to human readers, so too Cotton called his *Biblia Americana* a hive of biblical scholarship that he offered to the church for edification. Cotton transcribed long passages from all sorts of biblical scholars, including Catholics and Jews, believers and skeptics. Cotton invited all to the feast he had set; and throughout the book, rather lightheartedly, he guided his guests through a long, biblical, dinner conversation.

For Cotton the Bible was the coordinating center of a grand network of social trust between God and humanity. Christianity was epistemologically founded not on personal experience but rather in an extensive network of interpersonal communication about core facts. At the center of Christianity was the Bible, and at the center of the Bible was the trustworthiness of the eyewitnesses to Jesus' life, death, resurrection, and ascension. Working with the Holy Spirit through time, what is called a "communion of saints" affirmed the Bible's stories.

Cotton promoted the study of history because the history of people and events holds Christianity together. One of Cotton's most pleasant depictions of this is in a little sermon-book called *The Good Old Way or Christianity described appearing in the lives of primitive Christians and Ancient Church History.* In it he declared that "the *Idea* of Primitive Christianity . . . shall be fetched from the *Lives* of the more genuine Christians," and that he would fetch them "by raising the primitive Christians out of their graves and setting them in the midst of our congregation." Christianity, he said, is best known through reading history, especially reading the Bible. Cotton presented the lives and beliefs of those who had come before — the eyewitnesses, the testifiers, the first true believers — and told his congregation that these were the people they should trust, these were the "more genuine" Christians whose lives affirmed the credibility of the Bible.

Cotton embraced the reasonableness of social thinking and believed that a network of trust between God, angels, and humans throughout history was central to understanding "the experience of the faithful." In Cotton's form of biblical enlightenment, the reasonableness of social thinking affirmed the virgin birth. In the *Biblia,* Cotton noted that Mary asked the obvious rational question when the angel announced her pregnancy: "How can this be?" We too, Cotton stated, can ask "How can this be?" The truth of all Christianity hangs on a thread of information known to a young woman and the trust that her fiancé, Joseph, extended to her. For Cotton, the pregnancy of the virgin was "a mystery written in the scripture, as it were with a sunbeam"; however, "the experience of the faithful," the intertwined network of genuine believers throughout the whole Bible and subsequent human history, assures us of Mary's credibility and affirms Joseph's trust in her.

A favorite source that Cotton often referred to in the *Biblia* was William Whiston, one of the greatest Protestant scholars of the age. However, when Cotton learned that Whiston's reason had led him away from belief in the Trinity, Cotton was saddened that Whiston was succumbing to intellectual temptations of the age. Cotton noted in his *Diary* that he was vulnerable to such intellectual temptations. He recognized that his own devotion to wide reading among "criticks" had exposed his mind to trails of reasoning that enticed him away from traditional scriptural doctrines such as the Trinity.

This passage in the *Diary* is startling: Cotton Mather confessed that he was sometimes intellectually at the point of abandoning Christian orthodoxy on a core issue. His response to this enticement is even more arresting. There is no passage in all of his many writings that more clearly shows the craft of thinking in Cotton's biblical enlightenment. Tempted by his logic, Cotton responded with prayer. He asked Jesus and the Holy Spirit to keep him from error, show him his duty, and never let him "hurt any interest of God's kingdom in the world."

For Cotton, duty was of key importance to good thinking. In the appendix to the *Biblia Americana,* Cotton wrote an essay on one's obligation to the canon of scriptures. Good Christian thinking, he said, requires humility, and humility is the practice of submitting to the Bible. A pastor also must take into account the weighty responsibility of their position. Christian reasonableness is not the freedom to follow reason wherever it leads. Christian reasonableness is a method of thinking oneself deeper *into* Christianity, not *out* of it. When Cotton found his mind becoming beguiled by some clever but unorthodox thinking, he tells us that he went to his knees praying "that I may not mislead my flock in anything."

Winton Solberg, editor of Mather's *The Christian Philosopher,* notes how Cotton was intrigued by the unorthodox notion of the theologian Origen that all creation, even the stars and all humanity, might ultimately find salvation in God through the work of Jesus. Hell in this theology is temporary, not eternal, and Satan will eventually return to being one of the heavenly angels. Cotton noted that there is a passage by the apostle Paul in Colossians that "may seem to favor" this "high flight of Origen." But Cotton pulled back: "I recover out of my more conjectural prognostications!" There was warrant in Scripture for wide-ranging speculation, but duty restrains and sets limits. The overwhelming teaching of the Bible and orthodox tradition included eternal judgments by God and an eternal Hell. The reasonableness of duty demanded that Cotton not affirm the rather beguiling idea that all creation, even Hell and Satan, might be ultimately united together in eternal happiness. Only after the mind is properly secured in the Bible and the core tradition of the communion of saints, only then was Cotton happy to set the mind free: "O evangelized mind, go on, mount up, soar higher, think!"

For Cotton, the rationalist Bible scholars of the moderate Protestant enlightenment were not high thinkers. They were highly rational, but rather mundane in the way they did not let their minds soar free.

They gagged at gnats and let minor matters distract from the big truths. Cotton was the first important scholar in America to realize that a battle for the Bible was brewing among Protestant scholars. The traditional belief in the infallibility of divine testimony in the Bible was being attacked by those who insisted that the exaggerations, errors, contradictions, and historical contortions in the Bible proved that the Bible was merely a human book deserving to be analyzed as a human book.

Robert Brown in his *Jonathan Edwards and the Bible* describes how, in the generation after Mather, Edwards perceived that two infallibilities were confronting each other about the Bible. Edwards, with great subtlety and philosophical depth, saw that the rationalist critics insisted on their mathematics-like logic as an infallible tool in the service of truth while, at the same time, the Christian infallibilists upheld the trustworthiness of the Bible as divine testimony. Cotton Mather was not as philosophically sophisticated as Edwards, but he saw the same thing. He generically called the rational infallibilists "Sadducees" — people who, insisting on the power of reason, declared bodily resurrection impossible. In the *Biblia Americana* he presented himself as a reasonable Christian infallibilist. God, as the Holy Spirit, communicated infallibly in the Bible and guaranteed it as divine testimony.

One example of this conflict developed when Bible scholars in Cotton's era began to realize that during the Persian Empire editors had done much to cut, paste, and even rewrite portions of the oldest Hebrew Scriptures. The "Sadducees" used the evidence of these editors as a wedge issue to declare the Bible to be fallible and merely human. Cotton thought this was small-minded. In an essay on the Persian-era scribe Ezra that Cotton attached at the end of the *Biblia Americana,* he wrote that there was nothing in the Bible not "dictated" by the Holy Spirit, but of course that dictation was not necessarily a simple dictation to one person at one time in one authoritative language. Not only was an original author inspired, but so too were the editors and the various scribal cultures through which the documents passed. Cotton wrote that we should expect divinely inspired infallible scriptures to include all the sorts of logical problems normal to ancient texts handled by various scribal cultures over long periods of time. Cotton wrote that the Holy Spirit's dictation included inspiring a Jewish editor, such as Ezra, during the Persian period to rewrite portions of stories, revise information, change ancient Hebrew names of people and places, and, in general, make the Hebrew Scriptures more understandable to the

Persians among whom he lived. We should expect Persian political and social perspectives from the sixth and fifth centuries to be embedded in earlier histories originally written by Moses, or in the psalms originally written during the Israelite monarchy.

Sharply rational critics pounced on contractions in the Bible, such as Jerusalem being mentioned in scriptures that were supposed to be written before Jerusalem existed. Cotton advised his readers that we should expect in the Old Testament to find Jerusalem referenced before the actual city of Jerusalem was founded because divine inspiration of scriptures includes divine inspiration of editors like Ezra. For Cotton, the kind of scholarship that pounced on logical inconsistencies in the Bible needed to be lifted higher by the common sense of the whole art of being reasonable — especially the art of being reasonable when dealing with the complexities of divine testimony.

Two infallibilist positions tugged at moderate British Protestantism in two opposite directions. There was a hard mathematically logical infallibility on one side and a soft jurisprudential infallibility on the other. Cotton Mather in the *Biblia Americana* promoted the soft jurisprudential kind, the traditional kind that emphasized the source of the text in divine testimony. Jurisprudential infallibility was modeled on the courtroom. Witnesses take the stand and give their many testimonies. The prosecutor and the defense lawyer have a responsibility to cut and probe with sharp mathematical logic because the evidence is always weak and there are always doubts. The judge sets rules for who gets "the benefit of the doubt." The members of the jury who make the final decision are supposed to rely heavily on common sense and empathy. Juries have to try to harmonize everything they have heard and seek a consensus of understanding. The outcome of the court case is affirmed and acted upon as infallible, but the infallibility is soft.

Cotton Mather promoted this softer, more jurisprudential, biblical infallibility. In his *Biblia Americana,* Cotton recognized that a transatlantic battle for the Bible was heating up among scholars. He understood that it was not a battle between superstition and rationalism; in fact, he understood probably better than anyone at that time that it was a contest between a rigid form of rationalism and a more flexible form of reasonableness.

Eating the Bible meant ingesting a collection of books more sophisticated than any writings known before or since. The command "Consider carefully how you listen" entailed for Cotton also a command to consider carefully how one reads. This is especially true when reading the Bible as history. Much of it reads like other books of ancient history, but overall it cannot be made to fit a simple timeline. Rigid rationalism must be softened by what is to be reasonably expected from entangled communication between God and humans. God's story of salvation in the Bible was written by a God who sees all time at once. For a fuller understanding of the Bible one needed to use what Christian tradition calls "typology." Cotton's uncle wrote a whole book on typology, and there has been much scholarly wrangling about the subject in the history of Christianity. For Cotton, biblical enlightenment demanded embracing the typological tradition of reading that was first taught by Jesus and the Apostles. Jesus compared his coming crucifixion to Moses' sticking a pole in the ground with a serpent attached — all who looked upon it were healed. Jesus compared his time in the tomb to Jonah's in the whale. Paul talked of Jesus being a second Adam, and the book of Hebrews connects Jesus to the ancient priest-king Melchizedek. These were typological references showing that understanding history in the Bible required that the reader understood that a sovereign and purposeful God was integrating the past, present, and future in complex ways.

The story of salvation in the Bible is a story in which time folds back on itself like bread being kneaded. The fullness of time in Jesus is located at the center, while past and future times are organized to help understand the center. The Bible tells us that God sequenced the story of salvation this way for humanity's benefit. Cotton carefully extended Bible-based typology in traditional ways. For example, just as Paul states that Jesus is a second Adam (through one sin entered the world and through the other came salvation from sin), so too there was biblical warrant to read both the story of Eve and the story of Noah's ark as a "type" for better understanding the New Testament church. In general it was important for Christians to read the Old Testament as if it had the New Testament baked into it. Cotton felt this method of thinking had to be carefully handled. The Roman Catholics, he believed, had gone wildly astray with typology. On the other hand, obstinate skeptics incorrectly dismissed it as foolishly unrealistic. Moderate Protestants, Cotton believed, were tending to go too far toward skepticism and, in the name of rational simplicity, were ignoring typology as an important method of interpreting the Bible. One of the most important themes throughout the thousands of pages of Cotton's *Biblia Americana* is the proper application of typology. He offers illustration after illustration from throughout the Bible of appropriate typological readings. For Cotton, the Bible could not fully be understood without trying to read it the way God meant it to be read.

Was Nebuchadnezzar a Werewolf?

Just as Cotton Mather's biblical enlightenment encouraged a renewed blend of critical engagement with an infallible Bible, it also encouraged discovery of more knowledge about nature. Science in all its forms was fascinating to Cotton Mather, but he was most interested in scientific pursuits that blended his personal observations with information he learned from books — especially the Bible. Here again, the *Biblia Americana* exemplified his participation in enlightenment science. Out of the *Biblia* he collected many of the illustrations relating to natural science and organized them into a separate book published as *The Christian Philosopher: A Collection of the Best Discoveries in Nature with Religious Improvements.* The bulk and diversity of subjects in that book make it the most substantial book on natural science written in colonial America. In it Cotton declared that "philosophy is no enemy, but a wondrous incentive to religion." Using his expressive writing style he declared Christianity to be "a PHILOSOPHICAL RELIGION: And yet how *Evangelical!*" Independent of the *Biblia* was also Cotton's *Angel of Bethesda,* a book that has been ranked as the first important work in America on medical science. Cotton's role in promoting natural science in colonial New England cannot be denied; however, as always, his focus on biblical authority skewed his science away from moderate enlightenment to biblical enlightenment.

To read Cotton Mather's books is to discover why neighbors, visiting ministers, students from Harvard, and young men such as Ben Franklin enjoyed visiting him in his study. Cotton Mather was interested in everything and his curiosity was unbounded. He was a great guest to have at a dinner party or in a fireside chat. His knowledge of fun facts was endless — especially in matters of history and natural science. The *Biblia Americana* is packed with digressions such as: Was Nebuchadnezzar a Werewolf? Of course Cotton was not flippant about such matters. Such questions show the depth of his commitment to understanding the world fully, to having an open mind, to harmonizing diverse bits of information in the interest of offering a probability.

In the book of Daniel, Nebuchadnezzar, king of Babylon and conqueror of Jerusalem, is said to have lived for a period of time as a beast, eating grass and growing feather-like hair and claw-like nails. Cotton speculated that the situation might be scientifically explainable — that God had smote Nebuchadnezzar with some form of identifiable disease. The first possibility that Cotton identified was the simplest psychological answer: the extensive duties of a king made him susceptible to "a species of distempered and wondrous melancholy." But that explanation did not deal fully with the most arresting facts about his hair and nails. Cotton noted that there was much in Daniel's story that coincided with medical literature, both classical and contemporary, on werewolves. Cotton's scientific tone can be heard in passages such as this from the *Biblia:*

> Nebuchadnezzar's malady was not unlike a lycanthropy. A thing befell him like that which gave occasion to Ovid's fable of Lycaon and the story of Pausanias being ten years a wolf and then a man again. They that are under the power of this melancholy malady for the most part lie hid all day and go abroad at night barking and howling where they go. That such persons are molested with a demon is evident from Luke 8:27 (compare with Mark 5:3-4). And so, several possessed persons, which I myself have seen, would bark like dogs, mew like cats, clack like a fowl, and have manners like those of beasts.

The inquiry continues with Cotton drawing in more authors on the subject. From a historical point of view, Cotton thought it very possible that the Greek story of Lycaon being turned into a wolf by Zeus was derived from the rampant rumors passing through the ancient Near East about what had happened to Nebuchadnezzar. As a historian, Cotton followed Herodotus in the belief that the Greeks learned much from the literature of Babylon and Egypt. As for the medical science behind the story, we can see here in this quote a good example of the way Cotton harmonized scholarly literature, biblical history, and his own observations to offer greater context and understanding. Yes, God afflicted Nebuchadnezzar with something that we can associate with werewolfism (lycanthropy) — which seems to be a type of demon possession.

Cotton's open and synthesizing mind is also evident in the way he handled Noah's flood and the story of God making the sun stand still in the sky for Joshua. Careful reading of the Bible did not narrow the possibilities of what happened in each instance; rather, it broadened them. In a long section in the *Biblia* on Noah's flood and a shorter section on the sun's lack of movement, Cotton recognized that many issues of natural science were present in the Bible. Cotton believed the Bible had much to say about science and history, and that God was giving readers information of great importance. On the other hand, readers should not rush to judgment. Cotton reviewed theories of the flood and added that the Hebrew word for flooding the whole earth could be interpreted to mean a regional flood. Also, he noted, the Hebrew word indicating that the flood rose above the mountaintops might actually mean a flood that only surrounded mountains. As for the sun standing still, Cotton separated the experience of the sun standing still from the assumption that the whole solar system stopped in one position. Cotton believed that God worked a miracle in some way that caused the Hebrew army under Joshua to experience elongated daylight, but he did not think it necessary to assume anything larger. In both cases the Bible's account was true, but careful reading broadened the range of thought about what actually happened. Jews and Christians, he believed, often rushed to judgment and insisted on things that the Bible did not necessarily say. The Bible was always right, but Cotton always encouraged readers to be appropriately careful when interpreting what the Bible actually said about history and nature.

Very important here is Cotton's biblical understanding that matter and spirit are entangled and cannot be untangled. In Boston, a moderate Protestantism that insisted on separating matter and spirit took hold of many after the Salem witch trials. Thomas Brattle, Robert Calef, and others began promoting the claim that the witch trials had been the terrible result of irrational and unscientific forms of Protestantism. According to Brattle, "the reasonable part of the world" scoffed at the way the Salem judges believed witches could emit "venomous and malignant particles" from their eyes. Obvious laws of physics made it laughable to think that invisible chains could bind the arms of a physical girl — and that Cotton could cut the chains with a swipe of his hand. Brattle and Calef apparently believed in the virgin birth and resurrection of Jesus, but they believed that such wild mixes of spirit and matter had no implications for understanding events in the eighteenth century.

Protestantism throughout Europe had long been rationalizing the faith. Many Protestant scholars were promoting what came to be called "cessationism." The cessasionist position was that the miracles of the

Bible and ancient church were true, but that God had long ago stopped working in such extraordinary ways. Advocates believed that angels no longer were needed by God as messengers or agents in earthly situations. Instantaneous healings were no longer part of the divine plan. Certainly God no longer allowed the law of gravity to be mitigated by any form of levitation. Essentially, God had calmed down by the eighteenth century; laws of nature were being upheld, and the natural and the supernatural were being kept distinctly separate.

Cotton Mather found no warrant for believing God had calmed down. As a pastor who also served as a medical doctor, Cotton knew too much about the lives of people around him to think that God was no longer wildly active in and around New England. Cotton lived, preached, and published the biblical picture of a creation where the spiritual and physical intertwined. He and his church had experienced demon possessions, levitations, and angelic visits. He had been blessed by the Holy Spirit with his own ecstatic experiences. He had even heard about ghosts. In his *Diary* entry for November 1716, he thought the situation should be checked out: "There has lately been in the town, an apparition of a dead person. It is a thing so well attested that there can be no room to doubt it. It may be a service . . . to obtain a full relation of the matter, and have the persons concerned therein, to make an oath unto it before a magistrate."

Cotton's biblical enlightenment was open-minded to a wide range of experiences that moderate Protestants increasingly insisted were impossible. For Cotton there was no reasonable foundation in the Bible for assuming that miracles would stop, angels would cease to be active, the dead were completely out of reach, or that God would slumber into semi-retirement. Cotton believed that natural science should always be on the lookout for coincidences, remarkable providences, and obvious miracles. He, his North End church, and his "evangelical" following were confident that God was active and that he wanted to communicate in both normal nature and what appeared to be impossible events. Cotton read and approved John Locke's statement that miracles are an important part of God's communication with humans. He further assumed, along lines similar to Isaac Newton and Nicolas Malebranche, that God constantly empowers everything that is going on in the cosmos. Every work of natural law is a type of miracle because God is the power at work in natural law. What humans call miracles are simply distinctive evidences of God's abnormal activities that depart from his routine work.

Cotton preached and published that God is regularly interceding in nature with a range of remarkable providences, angelic agents, and direct miracles in order to affirm ongoing divine action and communication.

Cotton Mather investigated and affirmed miracles in New England in the same way he investigated the account of a ghost. Cotton was a great proponent of the importance of social ways of creating credibility for new knowledge just as social ways created credibility for science in general. There is a scholarly movement today that is reviving the study of social knowledge in the way Cotton Mather understood it. This movement is a version of what today is called postmodernism. Steven Shapin, a sociologist at Harvard, has written extensively on the way the scientific revolution in Mather's era depended upon "social truth" made credible by testimony and the authority of the testifiers. The leaders of the new science who were performing experiments and making precise observations were trusted, and today scientists are still mostly trusted, because of their personal reputations. The leaders of the scientific revolution, such as Robert Boyle and the fellows of the Royal Society, were trusted first as reliable testifiers, then, secondarily, their experiments and calculations were trusted. The scientific revolution began and still continues today as a network of trust. As is typically the case now, science was mostly known through social means. Most of us today believe that gravity has an effect on light and that speed has an effect on time because we trust the people and the books that say so. In the late eighteenth and early nineteenth centuries this type of epistemology was attacked by the most radical forms of the enlightenment in Germany; however, the wisdom in it is being revived today.

Two related tag lines that became important in the science-oriented enlightenments of the eighteenth century were "Mathematics is the language of God" and "Mathematics is the language of Nature." Cotton was not much of an actual mathematician, but he appreciated the idea that mathematics was infused into nature by God. Mathematics could be used as a tool to illuminate some of the hidden mysteries of nature.

Another of the important scientific developments of his era was the use of experiments. Here again, Cotton greatly appreciated the power of experiments, but did not perform actual experiments. The reason he appreciated experiments was similar to the reason he appreciated mathematics — God had created the world in a way that connected everything. If an individual experiment in one place illuminated something, then the illumination from that local experiment had universal implications.

Cotton, neither a mathematician nor an experimentalist, was of the more common kind of proponent of new science: a reader, compiler, and disseminator of what other people learned. Cotton's role in the advance of science in the early eighteenth century, however, was not only publishing books on natural science and medicine. He actually participated in great scientific issues of his day; but here again, we see a distinctive intellectual method to Cotton's work that is tangential to mainline enlightenment science. Being a social thinker, he emphasized the sociality of natural science and rooted his scientific thought in what was socially negotiated as reasonable. The best way to understand this is to compare how Cotton Mather and Thomas Brattle approached comets and epidemics of smallpox.

The differences between Cotton Mather and Thomas Brattle have been important throughout this book. The two shared the same classrooms as children, the same Harvard library as young men, and, as they matured, the religious and scientific hopes of their age. Both were thoroughly orthodox Protestants much concerned with the religious and political health of post-Puritan New England. Both of these men were leaned upon by Increase Mather, who recognized each for their different talents. Thomas Brattle exemplifies what is best in the Protestant interest of Boston and in the moderate Protestant enlightenment at Harvard; on the other hand, Cotton Mather exemplifies a new and hotter movement within the Protestant interest and a new, hotter, and more immoderate type of enlightenment. The two were both harbingers of future traditions and leaders of their era.

As for comets, Thomas Brattle, along with Isaac Newton, Edmond Halley, and others, held great confidence that mathematical relationships were fundamental to nature. Brattle, back in 1680, had performed precise observations on two comets going in opposite directions and assumed, because of apparent parallel trajectories, that the two were actually one comet heading toward the sun and then away from the sun. This was a radical assumption, and only two other mathematician-astronomers that we know of also assumed this. They were Isaac Newton and the Royal astronomer in Greenwich, John Flamsteed. Brattle was right, and his mathematical approach to nature was appreciated. Newton cited Brattle — anonymously as an "observer" in New England — in his *Mathematical Principles of Natural Philosophy.*

Brattle's mathematical thinking, which worked so well with comets, did not help him understand smallpox epidemics. In Boston in 1711,

Brattle searched for a mathematical pattern to describe the coming and going of smallpox epidemics. In this case his mathematics failed him. There was no mathematical pattern.

In comparison, Cotton also had a long interest in comets. He helped his father write *Cometographia* in the 1680s, and he later wrote an essay on comets that appeared in the *Christian Philosopher* and was subsequently republished posthumously in the 1740s. That essay gathered together the best writings on comets and directed his readers to the work of both Newton and Edmond Halley. But Cotton went further. He believed that God could use comets and other natural phenomena as a means to communicate general truths to humans. God revealed divine orderliness in the orbit of Halley's Comet just as he revealed a desire to love and communicate with humans in rainbows. When a particularly wondrous rainbow appeared over Boston, Cotton, thinking back to Noah's rainbow, called it "a spectacle and a sacrament which the Holy Lord has afforded and appointed for the encouragement of our faith." Comets were like rainbows: they were perfectly natural and, at the same time, were useful to a communicative God.

As for the scourge of smallpox, Cotton's most famous scientific success was in 1721 during a horrifying smallpox epidemic in Boston. Cotton recommended inoculations and even inoculated his children. He had read about European experiments with inoculations and his black slave told him of inoculations in Africa. The medical experts in Boston insisted that inoculation was a type of suicide, and in the furor of trying to stop Mather from inoculating people a bomb was thrown into Cotton's study. One of Cotton's inoculated patients was lying on a cot in the study when the bomb came through the window. The patient watched the bomb roll across the floor and breathed a sigh of relief when the fuse fell out. Tempers were hot in the midst of the epidemic, but Cotton succeeded in saving the lives of people who trusted him because he trusted the hearsay evidence of an academic journal and an African slave.

In short, both Brattle and Mather were exemplary figures of an early American scientific enlightenment. Brattle's method foreshadowed the mathematical-modeling that would prove highly successful in modern science. Cotton's method conformed to a social style of science that emphasized trusting experts and the character of credible witnesses. Both were approaches that advanced colonial American science.

Humanitarian Acts and Institutions, Freedom, and Liberty

Cotton Mather turned fifty years old in 1713, but he did not mellow with age. Throughout his forties he had only become even more zealous — sometimes seeming even frantic in his desire to attain his ideal of pastoral holiness. The character of his *Diary* changes around this time as entries become more like lists of good deeds done and to be done. This may be because the character of Boston was changing. War was descending upon Boston from the north by land and the east by sea. British officers and soldiers were seen more often on the streets and even at Harvard commencements.

Boston's population was also growing, growing in ways that scared those who remembered the old Boston. Imperial trade was booming. The rich were getting richer, and neglect of the poor was increasing. New churches were forming, but the docks were full of sailors desiring less than holy activities. New schools needed to be built, including schools for Indians and blacks. Good people needed to be organized so as to better meet the needs of the community. Cotton kept his eye on all this, and, as the leading pastor of the "evangelical interest," he considered these matters his special responsibility.

As was normal for him, he focused first on his neighborhood and worked outward. Out and about walking almost every day, always taking care for personal exercise, he took every opportunity to chat with North Enders. In these chats he would admonish the rich, give money to needy widows, and make sure every boat tied up at the wharf had a Bible on board. He carried small trinkets in his pockets to give away to the children playing in the streets — each gift came with friendly encouragement to pursue holiness. Many evenings and afternoons were spent with the private societies he belonged to and had usually organized himself — at one point he noted that he was a member of twenty such societies.

As was his lifelong bent, if he thought something was worth saying, he also thought it worth publishing. After finishing the *Magnalia,* he stepped up production of short books addressing specific issues. He often wrote one or two such books a month. One work that typifies these is *Orphanotrophium.* The Bible, he understood, has a special interest in orphans. The old Puritan towns had watched out for them by assigning them to families, but the post-Puritan seaport towns had lost control of the issue. Individual people and churches needed to step up to the need. Cotton passed the book out to the richer and more powerful people he met, and sent copies off to Professor Francke at the University of Halle, who was also concerned about orphans. Cotton Mather believed defending the cause of orphans to be an essential marker of a Christian society. Cotton himself embraced his role as stepfather to the fatherless children of his second wife, and at one point in his *Diary* he wrote of his desire to take another fatherless child into his family.

Cotton also remained one of the most diligent commissioners of the New England Company, the group that coordinated and encouraged missionary work among the Indians. Through this organization, he kept in touch with many frontier ministers even out into the Connecticut Valley. Over the course of his later years, Cotton took pride in his ability to converse with and preach to local Indians in their language, but he was troubled first that not many other ministers followed his example, and second by the realization that there were so many Indian dialects it was inefficient to try to meet Indian needs in their various dialects. When it came time to publish a third edition of the Indian Bible, Cotton joined with other commissioners, apparently in opposition to Samuel Sewall, in recommending that the money would be better spent on Indian schools and English education for more Indians. Cotton also recognized that the Indian dialects retained "a tincture of other savage inclinations which [did] but ill suit, either with the honor, or with the design of Christianity." Cotton believed that "the best thing we can do for our Indians is to anglicize them." The possessive use of "our" indicates that Cotton, in his later years, was settling into the British Empire's rather superficial view of evangelism among Indians. On the other hand, Mather believed that the "End Times" were coming soon, and his increasingly frantic social work was tied to his belief that he must do all that he could as quickly as he could. The efficiency of unifying the Indians in the English language was probably a step in his mind toward the globalization of Christianity that he was sure was soon to happen.

One of Cotton's most famous and influential books summed up his increasing concern for post-Puritan New England and the need for individuals to take more personal responsibility for their fast-growing society. Young Benjamin Franklin read the book and took it to heart as an ideal for his own life. The book's title says it all: *Bonifacius: An Essay Upon the Good that is to be devised and designed by those who desire to answer the great end of life, and to do good while they live. A book offered*

*first, in general, to all Christians, in a personal capacity, or in a relative,
then more particularly, to Magistrates, to Ministers, to Physicians, to Law-
yers, to Schoolmasters, to Wealthy Gentlemen, to several sorts of Officers,
to Churches, and to all Societies of a Religious Character and Intention,
with humble proposals of unexceptional methods to do good in the world.*

Cotton's humanitarian zeal often comes off in print as an obses-
sion. He always pressed himself to do more. He saw society falling apart
all around him. The North End was getting unruly. The rich people in his
own congregation were fighting among themselves for better seating in
the meetinghouse, and they competed for social standing. Centrifugal
forces seemed to be destroying what had been a more coherent, godly
society. Cotton pressed himself to do more, and it sometimes seemed
to him, in low moments, that God was not helping. God seemed to be
letting society fall apart. In response Cotton turned up, all the more,
the heat of his social zeal. Sometimes, he was tempted by doubt: maybe
all this organizing was amounting to nothing in the end. Maybe he had
dedicated his life to a false religion. Maybe the sovereign God of Christianity was not fully sovereign.

Writing about an occasion of doubt late one winter, Cotton worried
that he was diligently serving a God who unaccountably allowed "dark
things" to occur, who seemingly gave free rein to evil spirits and permit-
ted "ill things to be suffered." Cotton further worried that in thinking
these thoughts he might be falling into blasphemy, maybe even the
unpardonable sin.

After venting his fears, he wrote of the solace he found in humble
submission to the faith and in the realization that he would not be able
to understand all the ways of God here on earth. Someday in heaven he
would understand when he met God face to face. Feeling "a wonderful
peace in being thus resolved," he wrote of himself: "The flame revived,
and I went on with joy in my usual methods of a flaming zeal to do good
abundantly."

Cotton Mather's congregation, in a gesture of good will hard for
us today to understand, bought him a black slave. Cotton appreciated
the gift and named him "Onesimus" in honor of the Christian slave
and church leader in the New Testament. Jan Stievermann, a professor
at the University of Heidelberg, has written a long and powerful essay
on Mather's thoughts on slavery, the slave trade, and the freedom and
equality Cotton believed that blacks and Indians had the right to claim.
Although it was the Bible's picture of the reciprocal responsibility of

masters and slaves that led Mather to be confident in his ownership of Onesimus, it was more importantly the Bible that pushed him to condemn the slave trade and to promote the inherent equality and hope of freedom due to all humans, including Africans, Indians, and Chinese. Stievermann shows that Cotton's "radical scripturalism" pushed him to believe in "inalienable rights" for all human beings, which is the stated ideal of the Declaration of Independence. Radical scripturalism promotes universal human equality, individual freedom, and inalienable human rights.

This same radical scripturalism pushed Cotton to promote religious freedom for the Jews as a political responsibility of all nations in the world. Mather made this most clear in what he called the "Twentyninth chapter of Acts," an appendix to the book of Acts in the *Biblia Americana*. In it he copied over two hundred pages from a history of the Jews that had been written by a French Protestant refugee pastor in Holland named Jacques Basnage. Cotton read the book and made his transcription sometime between 1708 and 1710. In his transcription, Cotton upheld Basnage's condemnation of persecutions performed by Christians and Muslims against the Jews. He particularly criticized Christian heroes such as Jerome, Ambrose, Chrysostom, and Luther for their antagonism toward Jews. He praised Roman Catholic popes and medieval kings who gave refuge to Jews. This appendix to Acts is a global history of flourishing Jewish synagogues and academies on three continents, and the political leaders praised in it are those that promoted "tranquility" in their countries by insuring religious freedom: "The glory of a good prince," Cotton quoted, "consists in permitting every society quietly to enjoy the privileges they have acquired, and though that religion is not approved by a sovereign, yet he ought to preserve its privileges."

Cotton Mather viewed the world through Bible stories that promoted freedom, justice, and equality in the sight of God and governmental law. The opportunity to be educated, he believed, should be extended to all. Oppression of any kind was always bad. Cotton went further than most in applying these values to women, blacks, and Indians; however, as with sailors at sea, he did not think that their right to freedom, justice, and equality entailed the right to vote. He encouraged all people's opportunities for social mobility, but he was more interested in social stability within a system of reciprocal responsibilities. Onesimus turned out to be unappreciative, and Cotton helped him to buy his freedom. Onesimus, he thought, was spiritually and physically better off living in his household than in fending for himself — but the man must choose for himself. More than most of his contemporaries in New England, Cotton believed that God had conspired through history to give the educated British male the greatest human opportunity and responsibility for securing the blessings of justice, peace, and equality on earth. More than most, he believed that to whom much is given, much is expected.

Like many of the brightest and best of the intellectual leaders of the Protestant enlightenment in the eighteenth century, Cotton was interested in: (1) critical engagement with the authority of the Bible, (2) pursuit of more knowledge about nature, and (3) promotion of humanitarian acts and institutions along with aspiring to secure people's freedom and liberty. Although Cotton's form of enlightenment was neither moderate nor genteel, his Bible-rooted enlightenment was intellectually and socially progressive. He was a voracious gatherer of human ideas, experiences, and information, all of which were organized and governed by Bible reading, prayer, and the shared experience of the faithful. Cotton was not stuck looking backward. He believed human society and human knowledge should be getting better. The Bible encouraged him to think in terms of social goals of love and joy in which freedom and equality are promoted along with humility and mutual responsibility. Like so many others in the American enlightenment, Cotton believed in progress and steered his boat with hope at the bow.

"The Month That Devoured My Family"

On November first in 1713, Cotton baptized his newborn twins named Eleazar and Martha. These were the last of fifteen children born to him, and they would die before the end of the month. Measles swept into Boston, and Cotton made a list of its onslaught in his family:

> My wife has the measles appearing on her. We know not yet how she will be handled.
> My daughter Nancy is also full of them, not in such easy circumstances as her predecessors.
> My daughter Lizzy is likewise full of them, yet somewhat easily circumstanced.

My daughter Jerusha droops and seems to have them appearing.
My servant-maid lies very full and ill of them.
Help Lord and look mercifully on my poor, sad sinful family for the
    sake of the Great Sacrifice!

A week later, his wife dangerously ill, Cotton meditated on Jesus' prayer in the garden, asking that he might not drink the cup of sacrifice. He begged God "that the Destroyer might not have a commission to inflict any deadly stroke" upon the family. On Monday the ninth, his "dear, dear, dear Friend expired." He noted that his two oldest children by his earlier marriage were fond of Elizabeth, as were the rest of their children. When he had married her, she was a widow at age thirty. She came to him strong and mature. However, she seems to have taken some time accommodating herself to being the wife of a famous and passionate pastor. It was not an easy job. Pastoring was a cottage industry that burdened the whole family, and the North Church pastoral family was scrutinized by all of New England. Cotton loved Elizabeth and helped her deal with public expectations of her, but she apparently did not have Abigail's spark.

When Elizabeth died, the house was still full of sickness, even though the measles seemed to be passing out of the city. On Saturday the fourteenth the maid died. He noted the girl had been a "wild, vain, and airy girl" when she came into the household, but while living with the Mathers she had given herself to God.

Late in the night between the seventeenth and the eighteenth the newborn Eleazar died. Two days later, his twin, Martha, died. On that day also, Jerusha, his vibrant, nearly three-year-old daughter, was on her deathbed. He noted in his *Diary:* "I begged, I begged that such a bitter cup, as the death of that lovely child, might pass from me. Nevertheless! — My glorious Lord brought me to glorify him with the most submissive resignation." Jerusha died the next night. She had been in a coma, but at the last moment spoke. Cotton reported that she declared "she would go to Jesus Christ."

Cotton's wife and three of his children — within one month they all died. Winter was settling in, and he now embraced his remaining children and his black slave even more emphatically. To each he devoted more time, continuing their education but also pressing them to give their hearts to God in such a way that they might confidently present themselves for full membership in the church. He also threw himself even more fully into his work. At age fifty he was in his prime as a pastor and scholar. He criticized himself for wasting time and sometimes sleeping in. On a Sunday not long after their deaths, as December's cold and gloom descended upon him, Cotton asked for the grace to be a model to his congregation, holy in conversation with people and disposed to enquire into the glory of his Savior. He noted his attendance at the sacraments, his intentions of piety, and his many and various prayers. "My life," he noted, "is almost a continual conversation with Heaven."

CHAPTER 7

The Practice at the Top of Christianity

1713-1728

Winter Piety

Cotton Mather believed that the cold winters of New England could be good for people's souls. The "serious Christian" who fought the weather to get to church would be rewarded with "the more edification, the more satisfaction" from meeting Jesus in the service. "This is an observation often made by the People of God; the more the flesh endures, the more the soul receives." Putting on layers of clothes for protection against the harsh winds could remind them not to forget to "put on the Lord Jesus Christ." Cotton commiserated with his readers: "Truly there are in every winter many desolations," but winter could teach a family that Christianity was not simply a religion of joy, and God was not only found in happiness. Cotton advised his winter readers to be mindful of the invitation of the psalmist: "Come, behold the works of the Lord, what desolations he has made in the Earth."

Cotton wrote two devotional handbooks designed to be read by families during the long, cold winters of New England. He published several hundred short handbooks and sermon-books during his last two decades of ministry. Many were targeted to a specific sector of society, such as sailors or farmers, but most were of broad devotional interest and were written for the large number of literate families in New England anxious for easy-to-read, uplifting literature. His many funeral sermons about good women were published with an eye on the education of girls who would read aloud in kitchens while their mothers and siblings cooked dinner. Cotton wrote for all seasons and all occasions, but he was especially moved to write for the family that was hunkered down around the fire, snow piling up outside, with hands sewing, fixing things, and sharpening tools, while the children took turns reading aloud.

There was desolation during the cold winter of 1713-1714 at Cotton's house on Hanover Street as he gathered with his remaining children. The family prayers and discussions could not help but be bleak. Taking turns reading aloud could not but remind them of the family members now dead. In that house on Hanover Street Cotton's first wife, Abigail, had given birth to nine children but only four remained alive: Katherine the much beloved and much relied upon oldest was twenty-four; Abigail, nineteen; Hannah, sixteen; and Increase, eleven. Now his second wife, Elizabeth, was dead and of the six children she gave birth to in that house only two remained: Elizabeth, nine, and Samuel, seven. Together on harsh winter afternoons they would have all gathered in Cotton's study around the fireplace — the fireplace into which Hannah had fallen years before. Cotton would have had the family sing and pray together, but mostly Cotton probably kept them all at their studies. Abigail and Hannah would have overseen the work of the younger children. Katy had been fearfully sick, so she probably sat quietly reading a medical book. She was already much accomplished in Latin, Greek, and Hebrew, and Cotton, knowing that she was uninterested in marriage, encouraged her to make a particular study of medicine as a vocation. Increase Jr., by virtue of his age and the high hopes associated with his name, should have been readying himself to enter Harvard, but he dragged his feet as a scholar and his eye was on someday sailing away in a ship. His mother and stepmother were now dead and he had no interest in attaining his father's and older sister's scholarly expectations.

As for Cotton, we can imagine his mind wandering as he sat staring at an open book. His life seemed to be falling apart. Even before the family disaster in November, Cotton's church had begun to split in two. Also, Cotton was having financial problems. He might need to move the family out of his stately home and into a house rented by the church.

The good news about the church was that it was bursting at the seams with people. The bad news was that "seventeen substantial mechanicks" were upset about pew allocations and wanted to create their own church, build their own meetinghouse, and assign themselves the best pews. At that time, pews were assigned by church committee and the best pews tended to be allocated to the older families of high social standing. These "mechanicks" were men with needed skills, new wealth, but little formal education, men such as the bricklayer/contractor Ebenezer Clough, whose house is still extant and open for tours. Certainly they were justified by the fact that the Mathers' church could not continue to serve everybody in the fast-growing North End. The need to split the church could have been taken as a sign of success by Cotton; instead, he took it hard. To him, it appeared to be a situation like the founding of the Brattle Street Church. There was nothing wrong with splitting growing churches, but the motivation should not be the social prominence of a better pew.

During the fall, winter, and spring of 1713-1714, overt unity and propriety were upheld within "Old" North Church as the congregation officially broke in two. While still attending Cotton's sermons, those planning to leave formed a building committee and began to oversee the design and construction of a "New" North meetinghouse that would be built with a tower and steeple in the new imperial style. Those staying at Old North chose to counter the excitement of the new building by remodeling and expanding their own building. Cotton's emotions were twisted into knots, but he continued to lead both congregations through the break until a substantial number of his own congregation officially petitioned in 1714 to move to the New North meetinghouse. As with the Brattle Street meetinghouse, Cotton along with the other ministers gathered ceremoniously at the new meetinghouse to welcome the new church into Congregational fellowship. Cotton Mather always did the proper public acts of church fellowship, even when he was writing in his *Diary* that he thought Satan was behind what was actually happening.

As for Cotton's personal finances, we have no hard evidence. His first marriage had brought him into a wealthy shipping family. Following the guidance of his first father-in-law and brother-in-law, Cotton sometimes speculated in overseas trade by investing in certain ships and cargo. Apparently there were times when Cotton was rich. However, speculation is volatile and he sometimes lost substantial amounts of money. At any rate, Cotton was not much interested in holding on to money. He owned a fine house and filled it with expensive books, but Cotton seems to have given away much more money than he kept.

When he married Elizabeth and was cut off from the wealth of his former father-in-law, Cotton seems to have had a declining amount of money. However, he showed no interest in slowing the rate of his charitable giving. If anything, he seems to have thrown all financial discipline out the window as he pursued radical trust in God's beneficence. In 1706 Cotton calculated that he was giving away 600 books a year for free. From the *Diary,* it appears his book giving after 1706 increased rather than decreased. In the early 1710s he was sending book bundles to frontier pastors that included envelopes with money. He seems to have been a major contributor to any public charity that asked for his help. He apparently alone paid for the teacher and rent at the "Negro school" in the North End. In 1712 he gave the land for a new church to be formed in Hamilton near Beverly and Wenham.

Such financial abandon could not last. By late 1714 he was negotiating with the elders of his congregation to rent him a house. He was living on a pastor's salary, and he had an ever-increasing number of needy relatives for whom he felt a special responsibility. His house on Hanover Street was his major personal asset. He could sell it for a substantial amount and move into a house supplied by the church. The house he wanted was an older house a few blocks over on Ship Street that had become vacant and had long been a rental owned by one of his more wealthy parishioners: Thomas Hutchinson, father of the famous future governor and historian. On January 16, 1715, the church voted to rent the house and Cotton soon moved his household over closer to the wharfs. His own house was put up for rent and he later sold it in 1717.

A couple of months after moving into the rental, Cotton found what he thought would solve many of his financial and personal woes: a potential wife who not only was a rich widow, but also came with the highest of intellectual credentials. Her name was Lydia Lee George. She was a mature and beautiful woman, a little younger than Cotton. Her husband had died in November of 1714, and Cotton began to court her in March of 1715. Her credentials as an advantageous catch were so obviously good that she wanted nothing to do with Cotton. He would have to pursue her if he was to have her.

Pursue her he did. Even though she attended the Brattle Street Church, loved to wear fine clothes, and had no reputation for zealous piety, she was the daughter of Samuel Lee, one of the most important New England intellectuals. Lee had been a compatriot of Charles Morton in London's Newington Green, the famously dynamic hub of Puritan intellectual life in the 1670s and early 80s. Lydia was smart, well-read, strong-willed, and carried the aura of past Puritan glory. We know she was smart, because when she succumbed to Cotton's charms she insisted on a prenuptial legal agreement that gave him no access to her money. Cotton's undisciplined charitable giving was well known, and she wanted to protect her "considerable estate."

On June 24 Cotton signed the prenuptial agreement, and they were married by his reverend father — not by a magistrate in the old Puritan fashion — on July 5, 1715. In consideration of her move from the Brattle Street congregation to what was now called "Old North," Cotton preached a sermon in the Brattle Street meetinghouse. Over their thirteen years of marriage, Cotton and Lydia seem to have had long stretches of mutual happiness, but in general the marriage proved tumultuous. We only know Cotton's side of the story, but both had passionate temperaments. Cotton wrote that she would sometimes fly into a rage about his *Diary* and threaten to burn it. During periods when he thought her unstable, Cotton would hide his *Diary*. At times he kept a false diary out on his desk, while he kept a parallel and true one hidden.

Matters apparently were at their worst between 1721 and 1724. In 1721 smallpox racked the city, Cotton's daughter, Abigail, and a new grandbaby died, and Cotton was being verbally pilloried throughout Boston for advocating inoculations. It was during this outbreak that the bomb was thrown into Cotton's study. Lydia was at wits' end with her husband as he stubbornly pressed on. The household was in disarray. She probably felt that Cotton's children were supporting him and working against her. She had not signed up for this. Maybe to balance the household tension, she brought her niece into the house to live with them, but this only drove tensions higher. According to Cotton, Lydia's niece was "a monstrous liar and very mischievous person, and a sower of discord." Two of Cotton's beloved daughters eventually had to be moved out of the house to satisfy Lydia and her niece. In 1722 Cotton's father had a stroke. He died in 1723. On August 12, 1724, Cotton learned that he had been thwarted again from the presidency of Harvard. Cotton took this rejection very hard. He felt that many friends had abandoned him, and probably dragged his household down into his own self-righteous despair. Around midnight the next night Lydia went into a rage of "a thousand unrepeatable invectives." She pushed Cotton out of bed, and he retreated into his study. Lydia continued to rail against him, and Cotton was joined in the study by his seventeen-year-old son Samuel and twenty-six-year-old daughter Hannah, who had come back into the house. While Cotton, Samuel, and Hannah prayed together in the study, Lydia stormed out to go stay at a neighbor's house. Trailing behind her was her maid and the niece. She left in a "horrid rage protesting that she would never live or stay with me."

What brought Lydia back to Cotton ten days later was the death of Increase Jr., Cotton's beloved but troubled oldest son. Everyone in Boston knew that Increase Mather Sr. and Cotton were greatly disappointed by the young man. He was supposed to have been the leader of the fourth generation of the New England Mathers; however, the boy had proven to be no scholar, and, as a young man, not even a serious Christian. Their Cresy had gone so far as to father a child out of wedlock. But in the last year of his life the young man seemed to be responding to the prayers and encouragement of his family. His death hit Cotton hard, and Lydia came home to him. As best we can tell, Cotton and Lydia were reconciled until his death three years later. After Cotton's death, Samuel Mather wrote that his stepmother was a "disconsolate widow" and a "lady of many and great accomplishments."

All through the last decade of his life, Cotton was in deep financial trouble because of Lydia's family. Simply by granting a request from his wife's daughter, Cotton came to be dragged several times into court and barely escaped being arrested and sent to debtor's prison. Cotton, never pretending to have a head for such things, consented to administer the unsettled business affairs of Lydia's dead son-in-law. As an administrator to an estate, Cotton was responsible for demanding payment of unpaid debts to that estate. He needed to demand payment so that he in turn could pay the debts of Lydia's son-in-law. Cotton was pinched into a harsh financial middle ground and soon found himself the subject of litigation from both sides. His wife, intelligently upholding the prenuptial agreement, kept her money safely separate from Cotton — but by doing so, she left him floundering. Because he had foolishly — but with good intentions — signed certain documents, he became responsible for the estate's debts. He found himself being called into court, and furthermore being scorned for having to call people into court when he only wanted to have a reputation for being a generous and forgiving Christian. Eventually, threatened with debtor's prison, Cotton was forced to offer his one great financial asset for sale: his massive library.

Kenneth Silverman in his biography poignantly describes how in these later years of Cotton's life he suffered an "onslaught of diatribe and insinuation." He was "publicly, relentlessly, and ferociously clawed," even though he was a good man trying to do good. Bewildered by the reversals in every area of his life, Mather sat down with his *Diary* and prayed through his quandaries. He had expended much effort to support sailors, "AND YET," sailors slandered him. He had devoted much effort to helping the poor, blacks, and women, "AND YET," they scorned him. He had expended much time in the interest of his government and of Harvard, "AND YET," they were contemptuous of him. The list of these "AND YETS" goes on. He had long served God by being generous with money, "AND YET," he was now "a very poor man." Plaintively he wrote, "I have not a foot of land on earth, except a library . . . and this also I am now offering unto my creditors." And this was in order to satisfy debts that he did not create. He moaned: "My very *Library*, the darling of my little enjoyments, is demanded from me."

But God is merciful. Before the library was sold, four substantial men from his congregation showed up at the Ship Street house for a visit in the evening. Cotton does not name them, but he describes them as "men full of prudence and goodness." Ushered into the study and surrounded by the threatened books, the four men told him that he need not fear debtor's prison or the loss of his library. They would, out of their own resources, take care of his financial predicament. Cotton would die poor leaving a rich wife. But up to his last breath, he remained solvent and kept his beloved library. Most importantly, he remained the beloved pastor of his congregation.

After the new church had split off in 1714, his meetinghouse quickly filled back to its capacity of 1500 with those who wanted to hear his preaching. Most importantly for Cotton, thirty-five new members stood before the congregation that year and testified to their sense of the saving grace of Jesus. These became full members of the church that year. Gaining full membership was a serious matter that involved the whole congregation hearing a person's heartfelt testimony. Cotton rated the effectiveness of his ministry in two ways. The first, but lesser way, was simply his ongoing popularity as a preacher. The crowds who wanted to listen to him preach the gospel never waned. Second, but more important, was the steady stream of men and women, rich and poor, joining his church as full members. He, and others in New England, called new members their "harvest," and Cotton had steady harvests. After the thirty-five members in 1714, the yearly numbers ran twenty-four in 1715, twenty-one in 1716, eighteen in 1717, twenty-six in 1718, and fifteen in 1719. The year after his father died and Cotton fully assumed the senior pastorate, fifty-three declared their faith. In 1727, the final full year of his ministry, seventy-one new members declared their faith, the highest annual number yet at North Church.

Cotton feared that his financial and legal struggles would hurt his ministry. He worried that his wife's volatility and their separation would hurt his ministry. He worried that the new young Anglican priest in the North End who regularly criticized him would hurt his ministry. But, overall, Cotton's ministry remained strong to the end. God continued to use him, and he remained anxious to be used.

An Accomplished Singer

Protestants are at their best when singing, and Cotton Mather loved to sing. At night he would sing with his children and servants before sending them to bed. He would then sing with his wife in bed. He often sang alone in his study as part of his daily devotions. He believed that God created and encouraged singing. Cotton declared singing psalms to be "the united employment of our best powers and passions, in a most regular and perfect manner, for the highest and most worthy ends. It is public and solemn homage to God and an open profession of our allegiance to him before men." Singing, he continued, "is likewise a very moving and impressive exercise, carries a most powerful charm, and strangely reigns over the affections and passions. It is wonderfully fitted to brighten the mind and warm the heart, to enliven and refresh all our powers and cherish every holy frame, to calm and silence out evil noisy passions, to actuate and invigorate pious and devotional affections."

As with everything else he thought important, Cotton wrote books on singing. He also devoted much time to translating Hebrew psalms into singable form. He also advocated the use of musical notation to help his congregation sing better. He especially encouraged young people to study music. As was his normal course in such matters, after writing books on singing, Cotton organized his own choir. Young and old, but especially the young, were invited to form a singing society in the North End. At singing practice, Cotton would teach both the reading of music and the best techniques of linking words to music so that neither music nor words were compromised at the other's expense. At church services, members of his singing society spread themselves throughout the congregation so that the whole church would progress toward better worship.

Cotton Mather as singer and populist singing-master has been the unstated theme of this biography. In post-Puritan New England, many were treating Protestant Christianity as prose, while he was trying to encourage Protestants to sing. For four decades he preached, published, and called people to follow him into an all-day-long faith at the top of Christianity. Using the psychological categories of his mentor Charles Morton, he published, preached, and practiced hot rather than lukewarm Protestantism. During the 1690s and early 1700s he thought of himself as the sole leader of a hot-spirited populist party he called "the evangelical interest," a party seeking holiness when most of the other Boston leaders guided a lukewarm party he more broadly characterized as "the Protestant interest."

In this book I have emphasized the way Cotton Mather led a populist contortion within New England's Protestant culture that first fostered what we today can recognize as the American evangelical tradition. Cotton was conscious of what he was doing. He supported and encouraged a unified Protestantism, and went out of his way to promote the unity of Protestant churches; however, at the same time, he was unhappy with the lackadaisical Protestantism that was being fostered within the British Empire, especially within the empire's form of enlightenment. Cotton's loyalty to British Protestantism was deep, while his aspirations were high. The "twist" that Doug Sweeney describes as the beginning of the American evangelical tradition is an outcome of Cotton Mather's Protestantism being contorted by zealous piety and insatiable intellect.

Cotton never wanted there to be a twist. He wanted a unified Protestant fellowship focused on essentials. Musing one night how he might defend, restore, and revive the Protestant religion, he asked himself, what are the central *protestations* of Protestants, to what do they all testify? He came up with two essentials:

I. That the sacred scriptures are the rule, and sufficient rule, for faith, and worship, and manners to the people of God.
II. That there are plain scriptures enough to explain the obscure ones, and every Christian has the right of explaining them for himself.

Here was the foundation for a global Protestantism: God and man in communication, mediated by the Bible, with the individual rights accorded to every Christian. This was a Protestantism that could include

Quakers, Baptists, Presbyterians, Congregationalists, and Anglicans. It was a Protestantism that allowed conscientious individuals to differ about a wide range of theologies, worship forms, and ecclesiastical structures.

The tension in it for Cotton was that minimalist Protestantism could be believed by the lukewarm. He wanted more from Protestantism. He wanted believers to have a hot, passionate faith. He wanted people to live on earth in a heavenly way. One of his best and most characteristic books is *Coelestinus,* written when his father was dying. It promoted a heavenly perspective, not a minimalist, earthly perspective.

Cotton Mather died on February 13, 1728. He was sixty-five years old. Samuel Mather wrote at the end of his biography of his father: "From the Thursday before to that time he was dying of a hard cough and a suffocating asthma with a fever; but he felt no great pain. He had the sweet composure and easy departure for which he had entreated so often and fervently the sovereign disposer of all things."

At the time, Samuel Mather, Elizabeth's son, was twenty-two years old. Out of fifteen children, only Samuel and his fire-scarred step-sister Hannah lived to see their father die. Soon after the funeral, Samuel quickly compiled a biography using Cotton's *Diary,* a few other publications, and his own memories. Cotton Mather's passing was a major event in New England. Benjamin Colman in the Brattle Street meetinghouse and Thomas Prince in the South meetinghouse preached funeral sermons praising Cotton for his intellect, piety, social concern, and general affability. Colman and Prince were prominent ministers in their own right, but each considered Cotton to be the jewel in the crown of New England. For both, but Prince especially, Cotton Mather was an extraordinary pastor-scholar-mentor. Both of their sermons were quickly published and widely read. Peter Pelham had painted a portrait of Cotton the year before, and people, even people unrelated to the Mather family, were purchasing and ordering mezzotint copies to hang in their houses. Cotton was revered throughout New England.

Samuel Mather let it be known that he was writing a book-length biography of his father, and pre-publication purchases poured in. Samuel published a list of 303 pre-paid subscribers to the biography that included all the major pastors of New England and many government officials. A surprising number of subscribers ordered two or four copies to give to friends and pass around their towns. A surprising number of booksellers appear on the list ordering seven or fourteen copies. Entrepreneurs knew that there were many buyers anxious to read about the famous pastor. Several church libraries bought a copy. Isaac Greenwood, the Hollis Professor of Mathematics at Harvard College, ordered two copies. He had grown up in Cotton's church, was encouraged to study science by his pastor, and Cotton recommended him to the Hollis chair. Five members of the Williams family, one the Rector of Yale and three being pastors along the Connecticut River, ordered copies of the biography.

Samuel Mather's biography was published in 1729 and was 160 pages long. It still remains the best biography of Cotton Mather in that every page is filled with long quotations of Cotton's exuberant prose. The biography, passed around by families, sold by travelling booksellers into every region of New England, available at church and pastor libraries, and used by ministers to inspire and inform their preaching, should be understood to be one of the most fundamental literary inspirations for the Great Awakening — a name coined and promoted by Thomas Prince, Cotton's closest ministerial friend in his last decade. Throughout the 1730s Cotton Mather's biography spread his core message that God is lively, social, and calling Christians to a life of holiness. In the biography Samuel quoted his father on miracles: "I see my SAVIOUR, doing illustrious miracles upon the children of men in their distress. I feel the *Power* of it in my own experience of divine works upon my soul." Samuel quoted his father on the wondrous activities of angels. He quoted his father's description of divine love: "the *Ecstasies of Divine Love* into which I have been raptured. They exhausted my spirits. They made me faint. They were insupportable. I was forced to withdraw from them lest the raptures should make me swoon away." In 1743 an English edition of the biography was promoted by Isaac Watts. The English edition was much trimmed down and excised Cotton's wilder thoughts about miracles and angels, but it still rang full of Cotton's zeal for holiness. The shorter version of the biography was reprinted in America again in 1829 to help encourage the revivals of that century.

Cotton Mather's influence radiated throughout New England during the post-Puritan decades when the British Empire was establishing Protestant stability and the enlightenment was beginning to take root. We will never be able to count how many families throughout America in the 1710s, 20s, and 30s were reading Cotton Mather's biography and his many unbound, pamphlet-like sermon-books. The sermon-books, passed as they were among various households, have disappeared with the other ephemeral literature of the era. We know only that Cotton distributed them widely. He was a shameless promoter of his own personal mix of effusive piety and biblical scholarship. He commissioned ship captains to deliver bundles of his books at Atlantic seaports. He himself sent bundles of his own books to Indian praying towns and to up-and-coming young ministers with no libraries yet of their own. He also sent bundles to friends in other colonies, asking that the books be distributed free of charge to interested families.

Cotton was especially interested that his books be read in the Connecticut Valley where his cousins the Williamses and Edwardses were bringing the gospel to the Indian borderlands. Solomon Stoddard, the dynamic revivalist of the Connecticut Valley, was married to Cotton's aunt. Many of the pulpits of the Connecticut Valley were filled by relations who much appreciated Cotton's emphasis on a vitally active spiritual world wanting our salvation, and much appreciated the bundles of books that Cotton sent to them. In 1711 Cotton had a particular affection for a young kinsman, Eleazar Williams, who had just become the pastor in Mansfield, Connecticut. Cotton took it upon himself to become the young man's mentor, and sent to him a large bundle of books culled from his own library as a seed to a library in Mansfield. When in 1735-36 the Holy Spirit began to stir up a Great Awakening, Williams's church in Mansfield was among those first fourteen or fifteen churches to experience the revival. In 1713 Cotton gave money to the Reverends Timothy Edwards in Windsor and Nathaniel Collins in Enfield. He seems to have simply thought it a nice gesture of support at the time. Jonathan Edwards was Timothy's son, and he preached his "Sinners in the Hands of an Angry God" in the Enfield meetinghouse.

Cotton was an accomplished promoter of his work. He believed in the power of preaching, but even more so in the power of printed sermons, devotional handbooks, and short inspirational biographies. At the time of his death he was not only the most famous preacher in New England, he was also the most popular writer in New England. His son's biography of him, widely read aloud in kitchens and silently in pastors' studies, further enhanced Cotton's reputation and set the standard for a model pastor. A pastor should be passionately in conversation with God, committed absolutely to the Bible, full of piety, anxious to do good, and devoted to preaching the gospel.

This book, with modern binding and preserved in the Congregational Library in Boston, is typical of the many sermon-books published by Cotton Mather. He took personal pride in writing many books targeted for women, most of them funeral sermons. New England Puritans had long encouraged family literacy and taking turns reading aloud to one another. Books such as this one would have been read in the kitchen to mothers and siblings by girls practicing their reading. Normally such a book did not survive many readings and would eventually fall apart and be discarded. This particular book honored Cotton Mather's beloved daughter: *Victorina: A Sermon Preach'd on the Decease and at the Desire of Mrs. Katherine Mather* (1717). Although it says "Mrs.," Katherine (Katy) was unmarried and very talented. A biographical sketch by "another hand" is attached to Cotton's funeral sermon and tells how Katherine had learned Latin, Greek, and Hebrew from her father, and was an accomplished and pious scholar. Before she died she had decided she did not want to marry. Cotton was therefore having her read medical books and encouraging her to become a doctor.

(Courtesy of the Congregational Library, Boston)

A Burning Bush

Hannah Mather Crocker, Cotton Mather's granddaughter and Samuel Mather's daughter, writing in the 1820s in her *Reminisces and Traditions of Boston,* told the story of Benjamin Franklin's visit to the pastor's study on Ship Street. Franklin himself had related the story in her hearing — her father and Franklin were both born in Boston in 1706 and later developed a friendship. Franklin claimed that it was there in the house on Ship Street that he "learnt to stoop." He said he had come as "a printer's devil" bringing a proof sheet for the venerable reverend doctor to correct. When leaving he hit his head and "the Doctor in his way of humor said, 'Young man, you must learn to stoop.'" Hannah then quotes the letter Franklin wrote to her father that the advice "has been of use to me through my whole life."

Hannah Mather Crocker, Samuel Mather, and Benjamin Franklin each revered the memory of Cotton Mather and appreciated his ethical wisdom. Hannah had grown up in a house on Moon Street on the edge of North Square — what she called Clark's Square. She had watched British troops tear apart her grandfather's meetinghouse on North Square during the Revolution. She noted that in the 1820s the large Cotton Mather house on Hanover Street was still in good repair but that the "old house" near the docks that her father had moved into at age nine was now a "low boarding house." Her father, Samuel, had followed family tradition and become a minister of the church of his father and grandfather. But after the young Samuel had written Cotton's biography and settled into his pastorate at North Church he had to be dismissed. Clifford Shipton, who wrote a biographical sketch of Samuel, described the situation gently: "it became apparent that what had been an open and liberal mind in his father and grandfather had developed in him into what his contemporaries generally considered to be theological laxity." Samuel had married into the family of Governor Thomas Hutchinson and came to be more interested in respectable Protestantism than in the winds of the Holy Spirit that still blew among the majority in Cotton Mather's old congregation.

Hannah, of all the surviving children and grandchildren, seems to have been the descendent most blessed with Cotton's insatiable genius. She was born in 1752 and embraced the republican spirit of her age. Although when she was thirteen she helped her Hutchinson relatives flee North Square during the Stamp Act riots, she later sold the Hutchinson

143

tomb and had herself buried in the Mather tomb. Just before the Battle of Bunker Hill, Hannah, at age twenty-two, smuggled documents on the Charlestown ferry over to General Warren. She stuffed them in her underclothes and dared British soldiers to search her. Like many in her class and generation she found the promise of liberty and the construction of a new nation best expressed in a mixture of Protestantism and Masonry. Barred as a female from becoming a Mason, she founded an unauthorized lodge for women with other ladies in 1778. The following year she married an American officer and eventually had ten children. In 1813 she helped found a "School of Industry" for poor girls. She wrote and published poems and essays on temperance, the doctrine of the Trinity, and in 1818 America's first feminist tract: *Observations on the Real Rights of Women.* Like her grandfather, she believed that the creation story in the Bible was the foundation for equality among all humans. Her Christianity, however, was of a foggy generic type. Her grandfather would not have recognized her as walking the road to "the top of Christianity."

Hannah Mather Crocker, Samuel Mather, and Benjamin Franklin upheld the memory of Cotton Mather, but they were most interested in what Cotton was less interested in. They were interested in Protestantism's social utility, republican values, and emphasis on equality in the eye of God. Cotton promoted these but was most interested in an all-day-long faith. Cotton Mather's legacy was best lived out in Joshua Gee, a North End boy who grew up in the Mathers' church. When Increase Mather died in 1723, Gee was brought in by the church to be Cotton Mather's associate pastor. The church expected Gee to be Cotton's successor, and five years later when Cotton died, Gee became the senior pastor. It was under Gee's leadership that Samuel was hired as associate pastor for a time, following in his father's footsteps. Gee did not have Cotton's effusive nature nor Cotton's extraordinary capacities; however, Gee's faith and his preaching were at the center of what Cotton had lived his life for.

In 1743 during the heat of the Great Awakening when pastors were choosing whether or not to support the revivals, Gee split with Cotton's son at a meeting of ministers. Samuel Mather was against what he considered the disorderly enthusiasm of the revivals. Gee was on the side of encouraging the revivals. For Gee, it was not the place of pastors to hinder the Holy Spirit. He looked at the pastors who agreed with Samuel Mather and saw a "worldly interest evidently gaining the ascendant over a religious interest." Gee feared the effects of their "lukewarmness." In response Gee declared in words reminiscent of the man he called "the venerable" Cotton Mather: "May God our savior more abundantly pour out his Spirit among us, both on ministers and people! May the Lord further appear in his glory among us, and build up Zion."

In conclusion, let us return to where we began: the pastor's study. This was the most active room in Cotton's houses — more active even than the kitchen. His children and other young people were encouraged to join him there. Students from Harvard were tutored there. Members of his congregation were encouraged to meet him there. His father and other pastors were invited to sit with him there. It was there that he wrote sermons while on his knees and clutched his son and daughter as his wife stormed out of the house. It was there in the pastor's study that he likened the Bible to the burning bush through which God and Moses conversed. As a young pastor in the study his parents set aside for him, Cotton had clutched his Bible and prayed that he would "love it, prize it, converse with it." The hundreds of books he wrote in his three different studies all taught this sort of wild abandonment to love, prize, and converse with the Bible. It was this biblical communication with a lively and social God that kept him from being lukewarm, and it was this "radical scripturalism" that rallied people to him at the beginning of the American evangelical tradition.

Acknowledgments and Bibliography

Acknowledgments

Many people have made this book possible. I appreciate especially Barry Hankins, David Bratt, and Mark Noll. My college and colleagues are very supportive. Reiner Smolinski, Jan Stievermann, and the other editors of the ten-volume *Biblia Americana* are my guides when it comes to knowledge of the massive bibliography by and about Cotton Mather. Alex Goldfeld of the North End Historical Society gave a group of us friends-of-the-Mathers a walking tour of the North End. I learned much from him. Doug Sweeney, Agnes Howard, Tim Wood, Ava Chamberlain, Robert Brown, and Rick Pointer read early drafts and offered welcome advice. Annual meetings of the Conference on Faith and History and the American Society of Church History have offered opportunities to learn much from experts on early America and religious history. Massachusetts is a wonderful state, and I appreciate the resources and helpful staff of the Massachusetts Historical Society, the Congregational Library, the American Antiquarian Society, the Houghton Library, and the Harvard University Archives. The Huntington Library in Pasadena, California, is not only a great research library but also a friendly place. The people at Eerdmans Publishing Company have been very thoughtful and helpful, especially Kelsey Kaemingk.

Thinking back to what made me first appreciate Puritans, I think it was an undergraduate class led by a young lecturer, Edward Linenthal, who is now a professor at Indiana University, Bloomington. He not only assigned Edmund Morgan's *Puritan Dilemma,* a great book, but also one day took the stage in front of the lecture hall pretending to be Jonathan

Edwards. I vividly remember him, robed and bewigged, reading to us in a booming voice "Sinners in the Hands of an Angry God." For 200 of us kids at UC Santa Barbara, this was an eye-opening experience. Edwin Gaustad was on my Ph.D. committee, and I remember him fondly. Harold Kirker, a gentleman-scholar, has been my mentor now for over thirty-five years. He teaches me still, as a Californian, to love New England's history, architecture, and geography.

Bibliography

The following is a short list is of important sources that stand immediately behind specific statements in the text. If you are doing serious work on Cotton Mather and need specific information about my quotes or statements, you are welcome to contact me by email through my university email address. However, most all of the sources listed below have many footnotes to guide your studies. One last bibliographical note: The witch trial material in this biography is in agreement with scholars who discount as thoroughly untrustworthy Robert Calef's *More Wonders of the Invisible World* (London, 1700). For an excellent summary of what has long been known about Calef and his misrepresentations of the Mathers, other ministers, and the trials in general, see W. F. Poole, "Witchcraft in Boston," in *The Memorial History of Boston,* ed. Justin Winsor, 4 vols. (Boston: James R. Osgood and Co., 1882), 2:165-72.

Beall, Otho T. Jr., and Richard H. Shyrock. *Cotton Mather: First Significant Figure in American Medicine.* Baltimore: Johns Hopkins University Press, 1954.

Benes, Peter. *Meetinghouses of Early New England.* Boston: University of Massachusetts Press, 2012.

Bernhard, Virginia. "Cotton Mather's 'Most Unhappy Wife': Reflections on the Uses of Historical Evidence." *The New England Quarterly* 60 (1987): 341-62.

Botting, Eileen Hunt. "Ascending the Rostrum: Hannah Mather Crocker and Women's Political Oratory." *The Journal of Politics* 74 (2012): 977-91.

Brattle, Thomas. His letter concerning the witch trials is printed in full in George Lincoln Burr's *Narratives of the Witchcraft Cases, 1648-1706.* New York: Charles Scribner's Sons, 1914. Pp. 167-90.

Breitwieser, Mitchell Robert. *Cotton Mather and Benjamin Franklin: The Price of Representative Personality.* Cambridge: Cambridge University Press, 1984.

Brown, Robert. *Jonathan Edwards and the Bible.* Bloomington, IN: Indiana University Press, 2002.

Cameron, Christopher. "The Puritan Origins of Black Abolition in Massachusetts." *Historical Journal of Massachusetts* 39 (2011): 79-107.

Corrigan, John. *The Hidden Balance: Religion and the Social Theories of Charles Chauncy and Jonathan Mayhew.* Cambridge: Cambridge University Press, 1987.

———. *The Prism of Piety: Catholick Congregational Clergy at the Beginning of the Enlightenment.* New York: Oxford University Press, 1991.

Cremin, Laurence. *American Education: The Colonial Experience.* New York: Harper Torchbooks, 1970.

Crocker, Hannah Mather. *Reminiscences and Traditions of Boston.* Edited by Eileen Hunt Botting and Sarah L. Houser. Boston: New England Historical and Genealogical Society, 2011.

Cummings, Abbot Lowell. "The Foster-Hutchinson House." *Old Time New England* 65 (1964): 59-76. Footnote 18 offers information about Cotton Mather's rented house.

Grainger, Brett Malcolm. "Vital Nature and Vital Piety: Johann Arndt and the Evangelical Vitalism of Cotton Mather." *Church History* 81, no 4 (2012): 852-72.

Hall, David. *Worlds of Wonder, Days of Judgment: Popular Religious Belief in Early New England.* New York: Alfred Knopf, 1989.

Hall, Michael. *The Last American Puritan: The Life of Increase Mather 1639-1723.* Middletown, CT: Wesleyan University Press, 1988.

Jones, Gordon W. "Introduction." In Cotton Mather, *The Angel of Bethesda.* Barre, MA: American Antiquarian Society and Barre Publishers, 1972.

Kellaway, William. *The New England Company 1649-1776.* London: Longmans, 1961; reprinted 1975.

Kennedy, Rick. "Thomas Brattle: A Mathematician-Architect in the Transition of the New England Mind, 1690-1700." *Winterthur Portfolio* 24 (1989): 231-45.

———. "Thomas Brattle and the Provincialism of New England Science, 1690-1720." *The New England Quarterly* 63 (1990): 584-600.

———. *Aristotelian and Cartesian Logic at Harvard: Morton's "System of Logick" and Brattle's "Compendium of Logick."* Boston: Colonial Society of Massachusetts and Charlottesville: University Press of Virginia, 1995.

————. *A History of Reasonableness: Testimony and Authority in the Art of Thinking.* Rochester, NY: University of Rochester Press, 2004.

————. "Educating Bees: The Craft of Humility in Classical and Christian Liberal Arts." *Christian Scholar's Review* 42 (2012): 29-42.

Kennedy, Rick, and Thomas Knoles. "Increase Mather's *Catechismus Logicus:* A Translation and an Analysis of the Role of a Ramist Catechism at Harvard." *Proceedings of the American Antiquarian Society* 109 (1999): 145-223.

Kennedy, Rick, and Harry Clark Maddux. "Introduction." In Cotton Mather, *Biblia Americana: John-Acts.* Vol 8. Tübingen: Mohr Siebeck and Grand Rapids: Baker Academic, forthcoming in 2017.

Kidd, Thomas S. *The Protestant Interest: New England after Puritanism.* New Haven: Yale University Press, 2004.

————. "The Healing of Mercy Wheeler: Illness and Miracles among Early American Evangelicals." *William and Mary Quarterly,* 3rd ser., 63 (2006): 149-70.

Knoles, Thomas, and Lucia Zaucha Knoles. "*'In Usum Pupillorum':* Student-Transcribed Texts at Harvard College Before 1740." *Proceedings of the American Antiquarian Society* 109 (1999): 333-414.

Levin, David. "Cotton Mather's Declaration of Gentlemen and Thomas Jefferson's Declaration of Independence." *The New England Quarterly* 50 (1977): 509-14.

————. *Cotton Mather: The Young Life of the Lord's Remembrancer 1663-1703.* Cambridge, MA: Harvard University Press, 1978.

————. "When Did Cotton Mather See the Angel?" *Early American Literature* 15 (1980-81): 271-79.

————. "Cotton Mather's Misnamed Diary: Reserved Memorials of a Representative Christian." *American Literary History* 2 (1990): 183-202.

Lovelace, Richard. *The American Pietism of Cotton Mather: Origins of American Evangelicalism.* Grand Rapids: Christian University Press, 1979.

Maddux, Harry Clark. "Introduction." In Cotton Mather, *Biblia Americana: Ezra-Psalms.* Vol 4. Tübingen: Mohr Siebeck and Grand Rapids: Baker Academic, 2015.

Marvin, Abijah P. *The Life and Times of Cotton Mather, or A Boston Minister of Two Centuries Ago; 1663-1728.* Boston, 1892; reprint, Forgotten Books, 2010.

McKay, David P. "Cotton Mather's Unpublished Singing Sermon." *The New England Quarterly* 48 (1975): 410-22.

Middlekauff, Robert. *The Mathers: Three Generations of Puritan Intellectuals 1596-1728*. New York: Oxford University Press, 1971.

Minkema, Kenneth P. "Introduction." In Cotton Mather, *Biblia Americana: Joshua-Chronicles*. Vol 3. Tübingen: Mohr Siebeck and Grand Rapids: Baker Academic, 2014.

Morison, Samuel Eliot. *Harvard College in the Seventeenth Century*. 2 vols. Cambridge, MA: Harvard University Press, 1936.

Nelson, Eric. *The Hebrew Republic: Jewish Sources and the Transformation of European Political Thought*. Cambridge: Harvard University Press, 2010.

Robbins, Chandler. *A History of the Second Church in Boston to Which is added a History of the New Brick Church*. Boston, 1852; reprint Bedford, MA: Applewood Books, nd.

Roeber, Anthony Gregg. "Her Merchandize . . . Shall be Holiness to the Lord": The Progress and Decline of Puritan Gentility at the Brattle Street Church, Boston, 1715-1745." *New England Historical and Genealogical Register* 131 (1977): 175-94.

Schlesinger, Elizabeth Bancroft. "Cotton Mather and His Children." *The William and Mary Quarterly,* 3rd ser., 10 (1953): 181-89.

Shapin, Steven. *A Social History of Truth: Civility and Science in Seventeenth-Century England*. Chicago: University of Chicago Press, 1994.

Shipton, Clifford K. *Sibley's Harvard Graduates*. Vols. 4-6. Cambridge, MA: Harvard University Press, 1933-42. Shipton's biographies of Benjamin Colman, Thomas Prince, and Samuel Mather are excellent.

Sibley, John Langdon. *Biographical Sketches of Graduates of Harvard University*. Vols. 2-3. Cambridge, MA: Harvard University Press, 1881, 1885. Sibley's biographical sketch of Cotton Mather in volume 3 is well organized, thoughtful, and extremely useful.

Silverman, David J. *Red Brethren: The Brothertown and Stockbridge Indians and the Problem of Race in Early America*. Ithaca, NY: Cornell University Press, 2010.

Silverman, Kenneth. *The Life and Times of Cotton Mather*. New York: Harper and Row, 1984.

Smolinski, Reiner. "Introduction." In Cotton Mather, *Biblia Americana: Genesis*. Vol 1. Tübingen: Mohr Siebeck and Grand Rapids: Baker Academic, 2010.

———. "Introduction." In *The Threefold Paradise of Cotton Mather*. Athens, GA: University of Georgia Press, 1995.

Smolinski, Reiner, and Jan Stievermann, eds. *Cotton Mather and* Biblia

Americana — *America's First Bible Commentary.* Tübingen: Mohr Siebeck and Grand Rapids: Baker Academic, 2010. See especially:

Brown, Robert. "Hair Down to There: Nature, Culture, and Gender in Cotton Mather's Social Theology." Pp. 495-514.

Dopffel, Michael. "Between Biblical Literalism and Scientific Inquiry: Cotton Mather's Commentary on Jeremiah 8:7." Pp. 203-26.

Gelinas, Helen K. "Regaining Paradise: Cotton Mather's 'Biblia Americana' and the Daughters of Eve." Pp. 463-94.

Kennedy, Rick. "Historians as Flower Pickers and Honey Bees: Cotton Mather and the Commonplace-Book Tradition of History." Pp. 261-76.

Stievermann, Jan. "The Genealogy of Races and the Problem of Slavery in Cotton Mather's 'Biblia Americana.'" Pp. 515-76.

Solberg, Winton U. "Introduction." In Cotton Mather, *The Christian Philosopher.* Urbana, IL: University of Illinois Press, 1994.

Sweeney, Douglas A. *The American Evangelical Story: A History of the Movement.* Grand Rapids: Baker Academic, 2005.

Thwing, Annie H. *The Crooked and Narrow Streets of Boston 1630-1822.* Boston, 1920.

Van Cromphout, Gustaaf. "Manuductio ad Ministerium: Cotton Mather as Neoclassicist." *American Literature* 53 (1981): 361-79.

Werking, Richard H. "'Reformation is our only Preservation': Cotton Mather and Salem Witchcraft." *The William and Mary Quarterly,* 3rd ser., 29 (1972): 281-90.

The Cotton Mather Trail: A Walking Tour in Boston Connected to the Freedom Trail

The North End during the Colonial Era

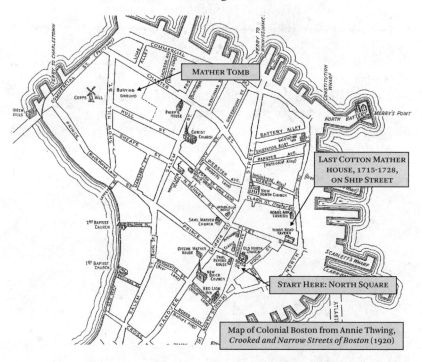

Map of Colonial Boston from Annie Thwing, *Crooked and Narrow Streets of Boston* (1920)

→ **North Square: Stand in the small triangular square looking at the Paul Revere House.** You are on the Freedom Trail, but you are also at Ground Zero for the history of the American evangelical tradition looking at remnants of Cotton Mather's boyhood home. The fireplace and overall appearance are probably not too different from the Mather house.

→ **Turn right and look at the site of the North Church meetinghouse:** After the fire of 1676, the four-square meetinghouse pictured on p. 69 was built here. Cotton Mather's granddaughter, who lived down Moon Street on your right, watched the meetinghouse get torn down by the British during the Revolution. In the 1690s, when Cotton began to flourish here, the church was probably the largest Protestant congregation in America, and North Square was the wealthiest and most powerful neighborhood north of Mexico. To your right is Sacred Heart Church. Read the information posted on the wall about it being the Seaman's Bethel, a mission to sailors in the tradition of Cotton Mather. Read the plaque about the Sicilian missionaries sent to the North End in 1887. North Square has a long tradition of Christian evangelism.

→ **Walk to your left to the corner of Prince Street and Hanover Street. Look to the left:** Across the street you will see Café Vittoria and Mike's Pastry at 294 and 300 Hanover. This is the site of Cotton's house that he owned from 1688 to 1717, which is depicted on p. 48. This is the home in which the two demon-possessed girls, Martha Goodwin and Mercy Short, were healed, where his daughter Hannah fell into the fire, and two of his wives, Abigail and Elizabeth, gave birth to his fifteen children. In this house he watched his two wives and nine of his children die. The house was torn down in 1882.

→ **Turn right and walk north on Hanover Street, stop before crossing Fleet Street.** Across the street, above the corner of N. Bennet and Hanover, is the site of Increase Mather's second house. In this house, Cotton had his first "pastor's study" after graduating from college. Just down Bennet Street to the left is the site of the church that Samuel Mather, Cotton's son, led after he was forced out of Old North Church.

→ **Note the name of Hanover Street.** Its name honors the first Hanoverian king, George I, who took the throne in 1714. Cotton Mather rejoiced at that time because he believed that the reign of the Hanovers would secure the British Empire in its Protestantism. In America, most place-names honoring British royalty were changed during and after the Revolution. This street's name is a remnant of Cotton Mather's era, even after independence and the North End's newer embrace of Italian-Roman Catholic culture.

→ **Turn right and walk down Fleet Street. Turn right on Garden Court and proceed to the Hutchinson House plaque on the wall halfway down Garden Court.** This short street that ran down the west side of the North Church meetinghouse was probably the most fashionable street in British America during the first twenty years of Cotton's ministry in North Square. Cotton's son, Samuel, married into the Hutchinson family, and Cotton's granddaughter, Hannah, helped her grandfather, Governor Thomas Hutchinson, flee this house during the Stamp Act riots. See the drawing on p. 48.

→ **Return to Fleet Street, turn right and walk to North Street. Turn left on North Street.** In Cotton Mather's lifetime, the right side of this street was all wharfs, and he spent much time down here talking with sailors, handing out copies of his books, and making sure each ship had a copy of the Bible. He targeted several of his books to sailors and fishermen. This street used to be named "Ship," and the house Cotton Mather rented was somewhere along the left side. In that house young Benjamin Franklin, the printer's apprentice, visited him and was told to "Stoop!" Cotton Mather died here.

→ **Turn left off of North Street onto Clark Street. Follow Clark back to Hanover Street. At St. Stephen's Church you are at the site of the "New North" meetinghouse** that broke from Cotton's "Old North" meetinghouse because the North End needed more pew space. Cotton was not happy with the break, but accepted it and at times preached here.

→ **Cross the street and walk through Paul Revere Mall to the Ebenezer Clough House.** Clough built this house about the same time that he and other "substantial mechanicks" were breaking from Cotton's congregation in "Old North" in order to create the "New North" Church. Cotton thought that Clough and his fellow church founders were mainly interested in attaining more prestigious pews, prominently positioned so as to express one's social standing. The politics of pews was of great importance to many in post-Puritan Boston.

→ **Continue on to Christ's Church, the Episcopal "Old North."** This church was founded five years before Cotton died, and its young feisty priest despised Cotton. There is a bit of a spitting match as to whether this "Old North" or the Mathers' "Old North" was the tower from which Paul Revere learned of the British advance on Concord.

→ **Across from Christ's Church continue up Hull Street. Enter the Copps Hill Cemetery to see the Mather Family Tomb at the northeast corner.** The structure of this deep crypt with the monument on top was paid for by members of the congregation at North Church when Cotton's first wife, Abigail, died. She was much loved, and the congregation wanted to honor her. This is a good spot to think about the role of women in Cotton Mather's life. Although we have weak information about these women, being a minister is a cottage industry in which the mother, wife, and daughters all share the calling of the pastor. Cotton Mather liked having well-educated and independent-minded women close to him: His mother, Maria Cotton; his wives, Abigail, Elizabeth, and Lydia; and his "little birds" Katy, Nibby, and Nanny. He never knew his granddaughter, Hannah Mather Crocker, but she carried Cotton's genius into the era of the Early Republic. All of these women are buried in the crypt beneath this monument.

→ **Go on up Hull Street, turn left on Snow Hill Street, and stand in the middle of Prince Street.** Look to your right and you will see the route out to Charlestown and the Bunker Hill monument. **Note that the Charlestown Bridge you cross to Bunker Hill was, in Mather's years, the site of the Charlestown Ferry that connected the North End with Harvard College.** Prince Street and the ferry were part of the geographical backbone of Cotton's life which was much involved with Harvard. Also, it is down this street and onto the ferry that Increase Mather snuck out of Boston in 1688 with the help of Cotton. Charles Morton, Cotton's evangelical mentor, and Abigail's family lived in Charlestown. The two often walked down Prince Street to the ferry with their young children.

→ **Walk down Prince Street back to Hanover Street. Turn right and head toward downtown Boston. Make sure you stop at a North End bakery on the way.** Cross from the North End over the underground freeway. Cotton crossed ramshackle bridges at Hanover and North Streets over a marshy tidal strip where the freeway is now. Faneuil Hall was not built during Cotton's life. **Stand between the "T" station at Government Center and the JFK Building. Face the "Sears Crescent" Building at a place where you can barely see the State House and site of the Boston Massacre. You are standing on top of Brattle Square.**

Part II: Central Boston during the Colonial Era

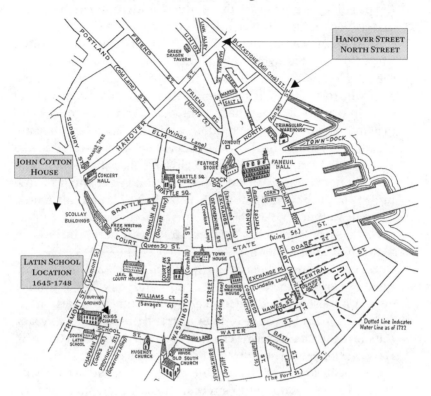

→ **Walk to the left of the "Sears Crescent" Building and you will see the Old State House where the Boston Massacre happened in 1770. Walk to it, and you will again join Boston's Freedom Trail.** The building that stood at this site in Cotton's day was called the Town House. Young Cotton used to walk from his home in North Square, through Dock Square (where Faneuil Hall is), past this Town House, down what is now Washington Street to go to school on School Street.

→ **Walk down Washington Street** and you pass on your right what long ago were the sites of Cotton's grandfather's meetinghouse and the site of John Leverett's boyhood home. **Continue walking past School Street to Old South Church.** Joseph Sewall was the pastor of this meetinghouse when it was built a few years after Cotton's death. The fear that Sewall expressed for this tower and steeple is the same fear that Cotton had for the earlier steeple on the Brattle Street meetinghouse (see the opening to chapter 5).

→ **Go back and cross over to School Street and walk up the right hand sidewalk to the point where you are even with the rear of King's Chapel. Turn right and face the statue of Benjamin Franklin. Look down under your feet at the mosaic honoring the site of the Boston Latin School that Cotton attended in the 1670s.** There is much to think about here and you might want to go sit in the garden under Franklin's statue. Cotton believed that an educated ministry and an educated congregation was essential to the long-term health of Christianity in the world. Throughout his life he was devoted to the ideal of Christian education. He personally subsidized a school for Black boys in the North End and heavily promoted the education of Indians. Ezekiel Cheever, the teacher at this school, was his ideal of a Christian teacher: one who taught his students "how to make prayers out of what they read" and was not "so swallowed up with other learning, as to forget religion, and the knowledge of the Holy Scriptures."

→ **Continue to walk up School Street to King's Chapel.** This church was built soon after the Puritan charter was revoked in 1688. Thomas Brattle is buried in the burying ground.

→ **Turn left onto Tremont Street. On your right is Park Street Church.** This church is one of the most important churches in the American evangelical tradition of the nineteenth and twentieth centuries. One pastor here was, at the same time, president of Fuller Seminary in Pasadena, California. Shades of Increase Mather, commuting between church and college presidency!

→ **Turn right and walk up Park Street toward the State House. Turn right on Beacon Street, go into the Congregational Building at 14 Beacon Street.** Walk inside and up the stairs to the Congregational Library. Sign in and ask the librarian to see the portrait of Cotton Mather. They sometimes have a display of Cotton Mather books. This library owns Cotton's manuscript diary for the year his beloved daughter Katy died.

→ **Coming out of the Congregational Library turn right and cross the street.** Walk a hundred feet or so and turn left into a walking area with Suffolk University on your left. You will see a ramp going downhill. Walk to the bottom of the ramp and you are in the old Pemberton Square. On your left is the beautiful façade of the John Adams Courthouse. Situated in the walking plaza is a low circular brick structure. This marks the site of the house of John Cotton, the grandfather and namesake of Cotton Mather. For us it marks the site where Cotton Mather was born and lived after he was first married. Here ends the walking tour.

Index

"CM" in the index refers to Cotton Mather. Book titles by CM appear under Mather, Cotton "writings."